LIVE RICH
AND
STAY WEALTHY
FOR WOMEN ONLY

by

Kenneth Himmler, Sr.

CEP, CRPC, CFS, BCE

Bloomington, IN Milton Keynes, UK

AuthorHouse™
1663 Liberty Drive, Suite 200
Bloomington, IN 47403
www.authorhouse.com
Phone: 1-800-839-8640

AuthorHouse™ UK Ltd.
500 Avebury Boulevard
Central Milton Keynes, MK9 2BE
www.authorhouse.co.uk
Phone: 08001974150

First published by AuthorHouse 12/14/2006

ISBN: 1-4259-2385-2 (sc)
ISBN: 1-4259-2320-8 (e)

Library of Congress Control Number: 2006901977

Printed in the United States of America
Bloomington, Indiana

This book is printed on acid-free paper.

"Whatever you vividly imagine,

Ardently desire,

Sincerely believe,

And enthusiastically act upon...

Must inevitably come to pass!"

Paul J Myer

My hope is that this book

will simplify and improve the quality of your

life,

and in turn, YOU will do the same for others...

-Kenneth Himmler, Sr.

-This is for the women reading this book that still have faith in the kindness of others-

A very amazing man with incredible gifts-the ability, the passion, and the determination to change the world, recently gave me an opportunity to be a part of this mission! His name is Kenneth Himmler, Sr. He is a wealth coach, as well as, the author of this book.

I first met this incredible man six years ago – and even then somehow knew that he possessed something within himself that was very special! I consider myself fortunate just to know him, and extremely grateful to be a part of this "movement!"

You see, Ken has been helping people-truly helping people since 1986 through an avenue that many of us find overwhelming-FINANCES! One life at a time, he has helped people improve the quality of their lives by offering his knowledge, his time, but above all, his compassion. I have witnessed him pour out his heart to help what some people in his position may have seen only as *clients*. Those of you fortunate enough to have already experienced his help-understand. Those of you that are reading this book right now are about to!

You see, Ken is a man who not only possesses a great deal of knowledge he is willing to pass on, but he will *only pass it on knowing that YOU will do the same!* Let me explain.

He not only wants to help you... *sincerely help you* **improve the quality of your life- He wants** *you* **then to help improve the quality of life for others! You see this book does not offer advice on investments. It does not sell or encourage you to purchase anything! The sole purpose of this book is to affect you in such a way that you will want to help others! YOU LIVE RICH AND PASS IT ON!**

This means that once you complete this book, you will have the knowledge to put together a team to assist you in reaching and quite possibly exceeding your financial goals. In return, you are to give back! You take a percentage of your wealth achieved, ONLY AFTER following the LIVE RICH STAY WEALTHY plan and give it back! You can willingly give it back in either the form of time and/or money to the charity of your choice!

That is right! The purpose of this book is not only to help you directly, but for you then to help others.

It only takes ONE person to change the life of another! This is the mission of this book! It is merely a tool to put this change into action!

The realm of possibility exists in all of us!

**WE REALLY CAN CHANGE
THE WORLD AND IT ALL BEGINS NOW…WITH YOU!**

*-Julie M. Berloni-(A woman that still has faith in the
kindness of others)*

THE STORY OF THE SAND DOLLAR

One September evening in Florida, there was a terrible rainstorm that lasted throughout the evening...

The next morning, once the sun had risen, a young boy and his grandfather decided to see how the beach had faired after the torrential downpour the night before. The young boy and his grandfather began their walk down the beach and saw that the storm had washed up thousands of Sand Dollars. They both were very cautious as they walked along.

Every few steps the grandfather was picking up *one* Sand Dollar and tossing it into the ocean. The young boy was very confused. Why, he thought, was his grandfather picking up only *one* and leaving the others. So finally, he asked, "Why?" The grandfather sweetly responded, "Well... all of these Sand Dollars are living creatures and they will all die here on the beach if they don't get back in the water!" Now, the grandson was even more confused! He said, "Why would you bother, there are thousands of them, you can't help them all?" In which the grandfather simply smiled, gently picked up a Sand Dollar, and said to his grandson, "but I can help this ONE!"

The young boy now understood, he took the Sand Dollar from his grandfather's hand, walked to the edge of the ocean, and gently tossed it into the water. The young boy then returned to his grandfather's side, held his hand and they finished their walk down the beach.

Many Sand Dollars were saved that day by the kindness of a young boy and his grandfather!

THE SAND DOLLAR CLUB

The Sand Dollar Club is a group of special individuals that have made a positive difference in the lives of others. This club exists so that we can publicly, as well as, personally recognize them for making a difference in the world, even if it is for only one person!

To become a member of the Sand Dollar Club you must meet all of the following criteria:

1} **After you read this book and you implement a plan for yourself, you agree to help at least three people; whether it is through time, money, or support.**

2} **You agree to either post your story on our Website, send us a letter to the address below, or email us so that we can share your inspiration with others.**

3} **You agree to either read the book "THE ULTIMATE GIFT" by Jim Stovall or watch the movie "PAY IT FORWARD" starring Helen Hunt, Kevin Spacey, and Haley Joel Osment.**

By becoming a member of the Sand Dollar Club, you will not only help three other people, but by sharing your story, you could inspire thousands! You will also be invited to our exclusive annual recognition event and will have access to special resources and benefits.

IN ADDITION, AT THE END OF EACH YEAR, TEN PERCENT OF THE BOOK SALE EARNINGS WILL BE GIVEN TO CHARITY. THE MEMBERS OF THE SAND DOLLAR CLUB WILL CHOOSE THE CHARITIES TO WHICH THE PROFITS WILL BE DISTRIBUTED!

560 COMMUNICATIONS PARKWAY
SARASOTA, FLORIDA 34240
YOU MAY CALL US DIRECTLY AT 1-800-983-LRSW-(5779)
You can also access many of the resources and our "Women Only" blog
by going to the following addresses:
women.liverichstaywealthy.com
www.liverichstaywealthy.com

MISSION STATEMENT

To improve the quality of peoples lives by educating and helping them to co-ordinate, integrate, optimize and organize their financial lives so they can feel secure and be free to live with peace of mind.

Enjoy your life

12. Optional – If you are going to work with a coach- how to find one.

⬆

11. Create a system of measurement and management

⬆

10. Create your list of actions

⬆

9. Create your initial plan

⬆

8. Create your gap analysis

⬆

7. Create your financial roadmap

⬆

6. Create your values and goals

⬆

5. Decide if you want a coach or you are going to do it yourself

⬆

4. Understand emotion over logic

⬆

3. Understand why a financial plan is needed

⬆

2. Create your business plan

⬆

1. Understand what your risks and challenges may be

Contents

ACKNOWLEDGEMENTS

I first would like to thank my three children, Ken Jr., Nicole, and T.J. They are the ones who have often sacrificed so that I may follow my mission. They have allowed me the time and concentration required to assemble this compendium of stories and knowledge. For their constant support, I am eternally grateful.

My thanks also go to my staff at Integrated Asset Management. George Lamarre, Chief Operating Officer, has kept everything together and allowed me to focus on my clients. He has kept the wealth management machine running smoothly for our existing clients. Jessica Miracola, my personal assistant, who manages and organizes my personal wealth, as well as, my outside business interests.

I also want to thank Julie Berloni. When this project first began, we had a number of editors and people with ideas regarding the book. Julie has taken over this project by editing the book, working with the cover designer, the publishing house, and working as the book publicist. Without Julie's hard work and dedication, the message and passion of this book would have never been this successful.

I also want to thank Jayson Harper for his creative and imaginative cover design. In addition, my appreciation goes out to Debra Lindsey for her professional photography and patience working with me. I also want to thank Dan Biondilillo for his insight, humor, and interjections with certain quotes used throughout the book.

Lastly, I thank all of the clients that I have had the privilege of serving over the years. While they have retained me to improve their financial lives, they have in fact, improved my life by allowing me to serve them and by being their most trusted advisor to handle one of the most important parts of their lives - their financial futures!

PREFACE

Congratulations! You have resolved to take control of your life and get your financial life on track. As a woman, you have probably faced some financial challenges along the path of life. Do not worry! By the end of this book, I do not expect you to be an expert at taxes, insurance, trusts, estate planning, investment management, and asset protection. Instead, you will have clear, concise goals and purposes outlined; a detailed, definitive plan, and the knowledge to assemble and manage a good team of experts, to be sure they are doing their jobs correctly!

In my experience, women born between the years of 1920 and 1950 are going to have the most difficult time. During these years, the rate of women at work was the lowest. [1]Women were more likely to be responsible for maintaining the day-to-day household operations, while men typically assumed the income and investment responsibility. This means that women in this era have virtually no pension plans.

We are beginning to see change, but will we ever see ***real*** equality? Men, over the last eighteen years have earned twenty percent more

---

[1] Feb 2000 issue of *The Washingtonian*

than women have! This is a staggering number, and even more reason to be prepared for the future.

Wise investing can assure you that even though there may still be inequality of the sexes in regards to the workforce, you can still come out ahead! A solid financial plan with clear goals and values can ensure your financial strength. Unfortunately, when polled, many women did not have a written financial plan. This is risky when you consider how difficult it can be to have a safe and secure future if you do not have a path to follow.

Come along with me and through this book, you will learn how to create your own path, whether you choose to do it by yourself, or have some help from a financial coach. ***This is the first day of your future!***

LIVE RICH AND STAY WEALTHY

FOR WOMEN ONLY

By Kenneth Himmler, Sr.

Do NOT EVER GIVE UP YOUR DREAMS...

AND NEVER LEAVE THEM BEHIND!

Find THEM, MAKE THEM YOURS,

AND THROUGH YOUR LIFE, CHERISH THEM.

Never LET THEM GO!

CHAPTER ONE

A WOMAN'S UNIQUE POWER

A woman's power is beyond measure! Typically, one woman plays hundreds of different roles in her lifetime. You have had experiences that have brought you tremendous joy and some that may have brought immense grief. Yet, through it all, you have gained strength, wisdom, and power! You have learned to remain strong in the face of adversity, rely on your wisdom in the face of uncertainty, and to harness your power or *unique ability* to get you through this wonderful, sometimes difficult life! You have learned, over time, that it is the experiences that matter above all else!

A large percentage of our clients are women and for good reason. We enjoy working with women who put a higher value on their careers, their families, and/or their experiences than they do on spending their time trying to be a financial expert. Every woman is unique and her behavior, beliefs, and attitude will have the greatest impact on her financial decisions. Our ideal client is someone who is too busy living her life to try to be a financial expert.

Why is this book specifically for women?

Financially speaking, as a woman, typically you are going to have a harder time than a man does. The odds are stacked against you. Here are some of the typical issues that you may be facing:

- ➤ Men typically, have higher pensions than women do
- ➤ Men typically, have a higher Social Security income than women do
- ➤ Men will die younger, leaving the woman to live on the existing assets
- ➤ When the man dies, the woman may lose the pension or receive a reduced pension
- ➤ When the man dies, the woman may receive a reduced Social Security check
- ➤ When the man dies, the woman usually has to liquidate taxable items at a higher tax rate, such as IRAs and/or annuities

Some of you may have already or are currently experiencing some of these issues in your life. Do not worry! Men may have some advantages over women in areas such as employment, but with the right direction, women are better equipped to succeed financially!

***A recent article by Jerry Miller in Financial Planning
Magazine stated:***

Merrill Lynch Investment Managers surveyed 1,000 investors-
(500 men and 500 women) in regards their investing behavior, beliefs,
and attitudes. Each of these investors also had at least $75,000 in
investable assets. Here is what they found:

> Women tend to be less knowledgeable about investing than
> men

> Forty-seven percent of the women **admitted** not knowing
> certain things about investments as opposed to the men at
> thirty percent

> Many women prefer to spend as little time as possible
> managing their investments, unlike men

> Women investors are almost fifty percent less likely to
> describe themselves as *very successful* at managing their
> investments

> **Seventy-five** percent of women also report being slightly
> more satisfied with their current financial situation, whereas
> **seventy-two** percent of men said that they were satisfied

> Women are typically less knowledgeable and enthusiastic
> about investment management than men, but women are
> more productive

- ➤ Women are less likely to cite greed, overconfidence, and/or impatience as emotions that have played a role in their investment decisions.
- ➤ Women are significantly more likely than men to engage a financial advisor.
  - o Women at seventy percent compared to men at only fifty percent
- ➤ Women are significantly more likely to have a financial plan in place
  - o Women at seventy-seven percent compared to men at sixty-two percent
- ➤ Women investors are typically goal oriented

What is going on here? The ***stereotypical notion*** that "***the greater knowledge and enthusiasm of men yields superior results***" appears to be untrue! What we find, in many instances, is actually quite the opposite! Women are reasonable, deliberate investors who make considerably fewer mistakes than their male counterparts. Few women say they are trying to beat the market *and* they understand the value that a financial advisor brings to the table. We have found that women, unlike most men, are open to advice and coaching. Just look at how most men handle taking directions. A man will typically drive miles out of his way before he actually admits to being lost!

Then, consider yourself lucky if he actually asks for directions at that point…most of them will continue driving determined that "they will find their own way!" Unfortunately, for us men, our ego gets in our way a lot! Therein a woman's power lies! Ego does not stand in your way of financial security. The even and planning-oriented approach and propensity of women to seek and take professional advice leaves them better positioned to perform over the long term. *You* ultimately have the highest probability for success unlike your male counterpart!

In the ensuing chapters, you will not only learn how to assemble your financial plan, find and work with a financial coach, but also how to automate your entire plan. Many women live their entire lives waiting for the moment when they can enjoy it. You might have riches right beneath your feet that you are not even aware of! **Don't wait to get started!** The longer you wait, the longer before you can begin to enjoy the benefits of this plan.

TOGETHER-EVERYONE-ACHIEVES-MORE

CHAPTER TWO

YOUR FIRST STEP

Your Unique Ability

Does it seem like we live in this world of *do-it-yourself* for *everything*? Maybe I just notice it more now, but when I turn on the television, log onto the Internet, or go to the bookstore, everything is *Do-it-yourself.* There are so many "DIYB" (do-it-yourself books) on the market. Let me explain why this one is different.

This is not a DIYB, but rather a manual of how to create your life's plan and then find the right team to make it happen.

Beware of the do-it-yourself books

If you are someone who reads DIYB, let me tell you why I think all those books sell so well, but do so little to really make major changes in your life. Some books, educators, and societies teach us that to be better people we should look at our weaknesses and try to *improve* them. I have tried this approach for the first twenty years of my working career, always getting frustrated with the results.

Many of us have two parts to our personalities, the technical side, and the emotional side. Just because you may be technically proficient in a certain trade or career does not mean that you will really enjoy it. In other words, you can learn all the in's and out's of investments, taxes, estate planning, and insurance, but will you really enjoy these aspects of managing your finances?

I know this is a very different approach than what most people try to do, but face it; all successful people have built their success with teams of experts. How many times have you seen a professional athlete get to the top of his or her sport and say, "I want to thank myself, because I did it all myself." You hear them thank their parents, their coaches, and their teammates. Think about all the multi-billionaires that have created their wealth through their businesses by creating teams. Do you think they did this all on their own? Do you think it was because they were experts in a certain trade, technology, or skill? On the other hand, is it because they had a vision, assembled good teams, and helped those teams execute their vision? I think you know the answer to this. They brought the vision and the team did the work!

Xcel Consulting

GREATER PROFITS THROUGH GREATER EFFICIENCY AND PRODUCTIVITY

By you using our new Expense Reduction Analysis service you will need the information in the book to learn how to handle the extra cash flow that you will find within your own company.

In the past, businesses with less than $100,000,000 in sales did not have the negotiating power to go to vendors and demand a lower price for products and services.

Now, with Xcel Consulting we connect you to an international company that has lowered expenses for over 6,000 companies worldwide. We do this by using a network of over 112 expense specialists that can help you lower expenses from:

Credit and Business Line of Credit	Computer Software	Cleaning Services	Building and Liability Insurance

Our no-risk guarantee says you only pay if we put money in your pocket?   Nothing gained – nothing spent!

Call our recorded line at 941-306-1787 and give us your name and mailing address. We will then mail you the pre-meeting form to complete. This will allow us to give you an estimate on how much we feel we can save you. You can also visit our website and click on the Contact Us form and ask for the pre-meeting form and we will send it out to you immediately.

If you contact us by August 30th we will enter you into our drawing to win a free IPOD Video. You can reach us directly at 941-306-4237. If you wish to order free information simply call our recorded line at 941-306-1787.

Sincerely,

Britt
Baker mtng. tomorrow
Jarold Childs
Thurs. mtng. 817-637 8227

Fleet Services	Workers Compensation	Employee Performance Reporting	LTL Transportation and Courier Services
Hiring and Testing	HR and Payroll	Health Insurance	401-K
Printing and Copy	Office Supplies	Equipment	Computer Equipment
Sales Tax	Property Tax	Packaging and Corrugated Containers	Advertising
Technology Services	Internet and Equipment	Office Furniture	Paper Products
Telecommunications	Utilities	Waste Disposal	UPS and FedEx
Temp and Perm Employment Services	Employee competency testing	Background and Drug checks for employees	Credit Card Processing and Merchant Services
Uniforms	Indirect Materials	Consumables	Transportation Services

OUR AVERAGE SAVINGS FOR COMPANIES THAT PARTICIPATE IS **23%** OF EXPENSES.

HOW MUCH WOULD <u>YOUR</u> PROFIT MARGIN INCREASE IF YOU COULD REDUCE YOUR EXPENSES BY 23%?

TEAM

Together-Everyone-Achieves-More

The human being is a complex, wonderful thinking machine. We get into trouble when we try to do things in which we are not experts or in which we are not very passionate. How much should you really know? Should you really know *all* the details? If you want your computer to print out a picture, do you care how the computer processor works or how the computer is built? No, you just care about getting the picture printed with the least amount of hassle possible. You care about the results, not all the technical aspects required to get the result. I am not suggesting that you just blindly turn over all your assets to a wealth manager before you really understand what the game plan is. The only way you will know the game plan is by reading this book.

Your Unique Ability

A focusing and time management coach named Dan Sullivan created ***The Strategic Coach*** and a concept called ***Unique Ability.*** It is not Technical ability, but Unique Ability. ***See, we all need a coach whether it is for your business, your health, your fitness, or your money.*** The concept of Unique Ability is based on the premise that we will tend to do things that we *enjoy* doing, rather than what we *have* to do. You may procrastinate on certain things, while you cannot wait to do other activities. Think about it this way. You have certain things that you know you *need* to do, such as run balance sheets each quarter, run income, and expense statements each quarter, learn the tax code to pay the least amount of tax possible, and probably a hundred other things when it comes to money. However, it does not stop with money. There are some things, such as, laundry, fixing the toilet, painting, etc., that you need to do around the house. You do not mind doing some of these things, but other things you just cannot stand doing. Do you ever say, "I know I need to do this, but I just haven't gotten around to it?" The tasks that you postpone doing are most likely *not* your Unique Abilities.

I have concluded that ***I am only good at certain things*** and other things I just cannot stand doing. **The truth is - I am just not good at these other things**. I will tell you that I do not believe that what I do, as a wealth management coach is rocket science. I really believe that you ***could*** do everything I do as far as understanding and managing investments.

The Kolbe Index

While in the Strategic Coach program, I was introduced to a concept called the **Kolbe Index**. The creator of this concept, Kathy Kolbe, created this new way of thinking. You can take their Kolbe

Index Test. It is what I call a tendency test. You take the test and it puts you into one of four categories. Each category defines what you will *tend* to do. Each person has a little presence in each category, but you will generally score higher in those areas that you enjoy. This gets us back to the point about the problem with DIYB. When you pick up a book on finances, it usually goes through new ideas and concepts that sound good in print. Nevertheless, look at how *your traits* will either hinder or help you when you are trying to get ahead financially.

You should only do the tasks you really want to do! The key is to find out what kind of person you really are and then assemble a team of people around you that makes up for your weaknesses. That is right! I did not say try to *improve* your weakness. I did not say learn about things that do not interest you because you have to. **You need to find out what you want - as the result**. Then get the team of people together that can help you get there. Dan Sullivan says, "The best thing that money has brought me is the ability to assemble teams of A+ talent."

Summary:

We all have inherent traits that we always gravitate towards. Unless you are passionate about money and wealth management, then find people who are. The money you pay them will be well worth your free time and they will most likely be able to make or save you more than their fees.

- It is good to learn as much as you can, but not at the expense of living your life and doing the things, you would enjoy.

- Do not try to be an expert at all things because you will soon be disappointed, which has the unfortunate effect of crushing your confidence.

Action:

- If possible, contact Kolbe Corp and take the test. www. kolbe.com Otherwise, determine what it is you really enjoy and hire out what you do not.

- Be honest; ask yourself, "If I had $10,000,000 would I really want to do this?"

- If that does not work, ask yourself, "If I only had seven days to live, where would I spend my time and what would I do?"

➢ **Decide now that you will put together a written plan with your values, your goals, actions to attain your goals, and a plan to obtain the right team to help you get there.**

1. UNDERSTAND WHAT YOUR RISKS AND CHALLENGES MAY BE.

SEIZE THE DAY

CHOOSE YOUR DIRECTION, THEN ACT
WITH ALL OF YOUR HEART. TOMORROW
BELONGS TO THOSE WHO TAKE ACTION
TODAY!

CHAPTER THREE

MY WEALTH, INC.

Your financial life is like a business!

Throughout your life, I am sure you have noticed there are some businesses that absolutely thrive! The owners can live a fruitful lifestyle with the homes, the automobiles, and the financial security of which we all dream. Not to mention, the peace of mind that comes with that financial security. Then there are those people who start businesses and always seem to be struggling.

We are now going to be talking about a company in which you are very familiar. The company is one that could be great if managed correctly. The name of this company is called MW, Incorporated. **It stands for My Wealth, Incorporated**. Not mine, but *your* wealth! Think about it for just a second. What is different about *your* money management from a business? Not much! A business has a balance sheet with assets and liabilities. You should have a budget, a profit-loss statement, and insurance. You should have a board of directors, a CEO, advisors, and coaches that help reach your goal. You should have a business plan outlining your values, your goals, your vision, and a mission. These are the beginnings of a powerful business. This same foundation should be used for your personal wealth management. Just keep thinking about MW, Inc.

Business Failures

Why do so many businesses fail? In trying to do the research on this question, it is almost impossible to put an absolute number on the answer because there may be many businesses that fail that we never hear about, or are not in the statistical records. According to my research, it seems as though most small businesses fail in the first five years. The numbers run from fifty percent to as high as eighty-two percent. Whatever the number, it is high! What we need to do, is to learn how certain businesses succeed and why others fail.

These factors have been identified; consider them when developing your personal financial plan. If you read some of the business journals or information from the Small Business Administration (SBA), they list *lack of capital* as the number one reason for business failures, *followed by lack of knowledge*. Many entrepreneurs come to the bank without any written business plan. They are unaware of how all the different moving parts are going to work. In fact, they usually do not even know how much the first year's expenses and income will be!

Relate this to your own situation:

➤ **How much do you need for basic living expenses?**

- Food $
- Clothing $
- Shelter $
- Transportation $
- Insurance $

➤ **What is the minimum investment return you need to get you to your goals?**

- Is it realistic and does it fit within your acceptable risk tolerance?
- What is your risk tolerance?
  (Not just conservative, moderate, or aggressive. How much volatility are you willing to live and sleep with?)
- What is your return-on-investment history over the last one, three, and five years?
  o In what should you be investing? What should your asset allocation model be?

➤ **How much insurance, if any, do you need?**

- What type and what are the specifications required?

- Should you carry long-term care insurance?
- If so, how much, what is the waiting period, what riders should you have and what are the specifications?
- Should you have life insurance, and if so, how much and what type?

➤ **What is your tax bracket?**

- Should you be doing IRAs or qualified plans?
- Should you be converting to ROTHs?
- Should you use a trust or other tax-shifting device?
- What are all the strategies that you should be using to reduce your tax?

➤ **How much cash flow with inflation will you need in five, ten, and twenty years from today?**

➤ **Should you create LLCs or other asset protection devices?**

If you have do not know the answers to these questions, it is like trying to start a business without a plan. When a person starts out in their first job, they usually have just enough to survive. By the time they get married and have children, usually the last thing they have time for is creating a written financial blueprint. Sometimes, people never get to the point of having a written financial blueprint and end up living a life of either quiet desperation or a life of insecurity about the future.

Types of My Wealth, Inc.

Let us take an example of two different businesses and you can answer for yourself what kind of My Wealth, Inc. you own. *The first example is about Mary and her new idea for a business, Mary's Hamburgers.*

Mary began working in a restaurant by starting in an entry-level position. She really wanted to own her own business and thought, how easy it could be. She thought to herself that she could make a much better hamburger than where she worked. She wanted to create the best hamburger her town had ever tasted. Mary set off to save up enough money to open her own business. Once she had enough, she found a good location and gave her first month's rent check to get her business off the ground.

Right away, she got a rude awakening. She never thought about all the details that her previous boss had to take care of. Unfortunately, she looked at making hamburgers as a simple business. However, what she found out was completely the opposite. She never thought about having to watch over and make sure the suppliers were not ripping her off. She had to file all the licenses with city, the state, and make sure she had all the insurance in

place. She was not sure if the insurance agent had given her the best deal, nor did she really know how much insurance she should carry. Then, it came to hiring a server so she could cook. No one ever told her about all the laws you have to follow when hiring someone. Mary finally found a nice woman to help her in her new venture. The next big surprise was all of the complication of payroll taxes. She worked very hard. In fact, harder than she thought she would ever have to. Then came the advertising and marketing. She had to get people in her restaurant. She had no idea how to create and run an ad and the best media campaign.

Mary had to do the job of the bookkeeper, the cook, the cashier, the janitor, and the dishwasher. Why? She did not have a business plan. She was undercapitalized and lacked the knowledge. As she continued, she felt, as though, she could never see the light of day. She was working eighty hours a week and she was just breaking even. Finally, she gave up and went back to work for a steady paycheck and steady hours. What is that saying about the grass being greener on the other side?

Mary might have been able to make the best hamburger, but there are so many other areas that she lacked knowledge. The same experience awaits some people when they try to become investment, insurance, or tax experts. People who manage their own money may do very well on picking the right investments, but may end up losing because of what they did not know about risk or taxes. They might have ended up paying more in fees, commissions, taxes, or lost the money due to divorce or lawsuit. In other words, they were good at making the burgers, but failed because of the lack of knowledge about the overall coordination of the plan.

Mary Burgers VS. McDonald's

Let us compare Mary's business to one of the most successful business models in history, McDonalds. Back in the early forties, a salesperson named Ray Kroc walked into a restaurant and the minute he saw it, he had his first vision. He saw an automated and process-oriented business that is now the largest fast food chain in the world.

Here are some of the facts about owning a successful franchise:

When you become a McDonald's owner, you are walking into one of the most successful process-oriented businesses that has been laid out and tested. I have eaten at McDonalds. Yes, I admit it. I have eaten there (the grilled chicken breast sandwich is good!) In all the times I have been there, I have never seen the owner. As a matter of fact, in all of the fast food restaurants I have been in, I have never seen the owners. Why is that? The franchise system is set up so effectively. You put up the money and their proven system of product, hiring, advertising and operations will almost assure your success. The most recent studies show that the average franchisee has a ninety-seven percent chance of success or less than a three percent chance of failure. Compare that to the eighty percent of businesses that fail in the first five years. You can choose to start and operate your own business and figure everything out on your own, or you can use a proven system called a franchise. What do *you* want as the result? Do you want the free time and lifestyle that a franchise offers? Would you want to work untold hours, take on high risk, and then, *maybe*, have a successful business? Why? Just so, you can say you did it on your own. I do not know about you, but I really would not want to try to reinvent the wheel.

This is the point of finding and hiring a wealth manager (coach); one that has a system in place to help optimize and organize your financial life so you can spend your time on what is important to you.

If you had to cross a minefield, would you go your own way or follow in the footsteps of someone who had already made it across? The best way to cross a minefield is not to be first! It is the same idea in business and in personal finances. Think about the overall comparison. If you are managing your own business - or your own finances, you have to try to figure everything out. You have to make all your own mistakes along the way, as opposed to putting together the right team of people who do this repeatedly and have already figured out all the mistakes. This type of set up allows you to ride on the coattails of their experience, like a franchise.

Yes, you will pay for this experience. If you own a McDonalds, you give the parent corporation a percentage of your gross revenues. If you hire a wealth manager, you are paying them a percentage of your assets on a yearly basis, just like a franchise. In either case, it is worth it to pay for the system of processes and procedures that have already been created and tested.

How does all this apply to your situation? I hope that by now you have recognized the parallel between your personal financial situation and Mary's situation. Your MW, Inc. is just like Mary's business.

When you are trying to manage all your own wealth, you are tying to be an expert in all the following areas:

1) **Investment management**

2) **Income tax**

3) **Estate tax, both federal and state**

4) **Insurance**

5) **Asset Protection**

6) **Retirement and cash flow planning**

The financial industry is a very complex and dynamic world. While you might be able to be an expert in one or two of these areas, what is the probability you can be an expert in all of these areas? After twenty plus years in practice, I am not an expert in each of the areas. This is why I hire experts.

A team of people can perform better than a single person.

Summary:

➢ **Education is not the only key to financial success!**

➢ **Look at the most successful businesses, they have a written business plan that is continually updated.**

   ✓ **You should have a written financial blueprint and update it annually!**

   ✓ **Create your business plan for your personal wealth management**

You can decide to try to invent your own system or pay someone else that has a proven system and simply follow it! Mary's Hamburgers or McDonalds?

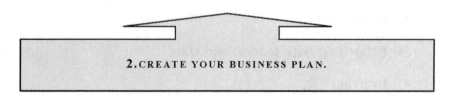

2. CREATE YOUR BUSINESS PLAN.

Notes

At the fork in the road, Alice asked the

Cheshire cat which road she should take.

The cat asked, "Where do you want to go?"

Alice said, "I really don't know."

The cat replied, "Then any road would do".

CHAPTER FOUR

WHY YOU NEED A FINANCIAL BLUEPRINT

From my own experience, the real reason that you need to have a current and valid financial blueprint is to have peace of mind. Many women create self-imposed fear and stress about the security of their financial future because they do not know where they are headed. By having a financial blueprint in place, that tells you how much you can afford to spend and how you should be investing, most women develop a peace of mind that little else can bring. (You will hear me use the term financial plan and financial blueprint. These terms are interchangeable.)

Here are some reasons why it makes sense to have a current financial blueprint:

An article in **Business Week** (printed November 21, 2005) stated, as of Nov 8, 2005, investors were expecting inflation to average only 2.6 percent annually over the next decade. This is the same rate as in the past. Expectations of inflation are at an eight-year high. **(Do** you know how much you need to earn to keep up with inflation after taxes?)

In the **University of Michigan's Consumer Sentiment Survey**, consumers predicted a 3.2 percent inflation rate over the next five to ten years, up from the 2.7 percent expected in January of 2004. Gasoline has gone up, taxes keep going up, college tuition goes up, and even in the clothing stores, where you used to find good values, they have even raised their prices. Inflation is not as tame as it was over the past ten years, says Kenneth Phillips, Chief Executive of IMPAXX, Inc."

Another article in **Senior Market Advisor** (October 2005), Dave Port wrote a piece titled, *Why Retirees Fret Over Finances*. When it comes to preserving their financial comfort, health care cost is the issue that most concerns seniors aged sixty-two to seventy-five, according to findings from Financial Freedom's 2005 Senior Sentiment Survey. Cost of living and housing costs were next on the list of issues that survey respondents see threatening their financial well-being, followed by the US Economy. **Do any of these issues ever cross your mind?** If so, do you know how you will fare with the increasing cost of medical care?

Financial Freedom Inc., *a reverse mortgage lender*, conducted a survey. Below is a list of the issues affecting financial comfort for some people:

- Health care costs: 64%
- Cost of living and housing costs: 54%
- US economy: 41%
- Taxes: 34%
- Investment performance: 29%
- Outstanding debt: 16%
- Family obligations: 14%
- Other: 5%

What is your opinion? What are the issues that most concern you? Do you have a plan in place that addresses your major concerns?

Depending on your situation, you may have other concerns besides the ones listed above. This is the reason why it makes sense to have a current financial plan. The purpose of the financial plan is to provide a safe and secure path to your ultimate destination. If you do not have a financial plan, these concerns and fears can make life miserable. You need to have an understanding of where you are going and how to get there.

Not only does the financial plan outline a road map for your financial future, but it also should eliminate the "What do you think of" (WDYTO) question.

The most common questions I get are, "What do you think of reverse mortgages?" "Ken, what do you think of the recent change in interest rates?" "Ken, what do you think of me paying off my mortgage?" "Ken, what do you think of me buying long term care insurance?" I call this system of financial planning the "**decision by consensus**". This means that you make decisions based on the consensus of whom you ask or where you get your information. Let me give you a great example:

In one of my classes I taught, I kept getting questions from the same person. "Ken, what do you think about the difference between variable annuities and fixed annuities?" "What do you think about reverse mortgages?" "What do you think about me buying life insurance at my age?" Finally, I had to explain that I was unable to answer any of these questions. *She did not understand that you could only answer these questions after completing a financial plan. After completion of the financial plan, you can do an analysis to see if any of these strategies make sense. Then you can compare the options to see if they would be a wise money*

***decision. One of the biggest mistakes you can make is to use the
old "Do you think that (blank) is good or bad?"***

Finally, I asked her what she thought of circular saws. She gave
me a confused look and said she really did not have an opinion. Then
I asked her what she thought of power drills. She asked me what that
had to do with her questions. I then explained that she was asking
my opinion on certain products or ***tools***.

Tools are only good if you have a blueprint and the goal to build
something. If your goal were to cut a piece of wood in half, you
would need a saw. If you needed a hole in a piece of wood, you
would need a drill. This is the same basic principle when it comes to
financial products. You must first have a financial plan so you know
which tools you *need* to use and which ones you do not.

One of the problems with financial products is that people put
a **GOOD** or **BAD** label on them based on what they hear or have
learned. The only ***bad*** financial products are those that a salesperson
sells you when it does not fit. It would be the same as if you wanted
a straight cut and you needed a saw, yet the salesperson sells you a
drill. Stop asking yourself and other people of what they think of
things. In most cases, you are asking people that do not know any
better than you do and they are giving you faulty information. In
some cases, people will give you this advice just to make themselves
feel important or smart.

This is the point of having a current and valid financial plan.

Do you have a compelling financial plan where you have outlined your values, written goals with target dates, dollar amounts and action plans to get to those goals? If you have a financial plan, no WDYTO questions should be coming up because the financial plan answers them.

Now that you understand the importance of having a financial plan, let me now tell you how they can fail.

Let us say you have a financial plan in place. Does that mean you are now living your life to the highest vision you could imagine? NO WAY! It is like the person who goes to the gym everyday and is still not seeing the results they want. Why or how can this happen? All financial plans give you the life you want, right? The answer is NO!

Financial Plans can fail for three reasons:

1) It is not your plan – it is a canned plan (This is the fault of the advisor or company selling a canned plan)

2) It is a product-oriented presentation – not really a financial plan (This is the fault of the advisor or company the advisor works for)

3) There is no commitment by you or the planner

Canned Plan

Many online financial planning programs enable you to set up your own financial plan. *In many cases, when you go online and create these canned plans you get the same result, a set of cookie cutter financial plans that are really not designed for the way you want to live.*

There are many low cost, **canned** planning software programs available. Why is this method a bad idea? Well, you would never consider taking out your own appendix, even though you can go and buy a scalpel at a medical supply store!

Product –Oriented Plan

Unfortunately, there are financial persons in the industry that develop plans strictly around products. You could end up with a plan that does you absolutely no good and with products that may not even fit your needs at all! Please understand that financial products are a necessary part of any financial plan, but they are not the financial plan. Think about all the financial products that we need. We need mutual funds, stocks, bonds, life insurance, long-term care insurance, health insurance, mortgages, reverse mortgages, fixed annuities, and variable annuities and, yes, even bank CDs. We need these products to make a plan work. Remember, it is not the tool, itself, but rather, the **result** the tool provides!

Plan Takes Commitment

Financial plans are like diets- they take commitment. Why do some people always seem to stay in great shape? In my non-medical opinion, I think it comes down to what you really enjoy doing. If you enjoy working out, you will most likely do it often. Good old willpower and discipline only last so long when you are doing something that you do not enjoy. Have you ever noticed that when someone has a personal trainer, that person is able to achieve things previously thought to be impossible? I have noticed many people who consistently battle with their weight and exercising. They may have a medical condition that prevents them from certain activities. I think, in most cases, they eat inconsistently and exercise out of guilt, as opposed to, committing to a healthy lifestyle with a plan.

Eventually, most humble people will realize the power of using a coach, but imagine what happens when you finally hire a personal trainer and they focus on their needs, sell you a canned workout or diet, or worse, try to sell you products. Unfortunately, this happens to many people dealing with financial services. You must know what you want from your financial advisor. What you do **not** want is an advisor that tries to impose their wants, instead of first trying to understand what **you** want. In some cases, people get a financial plan based more on what the financial planner wants. This is one of the quickest ways to have a financial plan fail, because it is not your plan.

The financial planning and financial services field is very diverse, complex, and complicated for the consumer to really understand. The government does not make it easier because it has created a fragmented system of regulation. Do not feel bad if you are having a hard time understanding. Later in the book, I will review with you how to find a good planner and how to set up a good financial plan.

Summary:

> - **Inflation will continue to be one of your biggest enemies in being able to maintain your present lifestyle.**

> - **Health care costs are skyrocketing and could be a potential wealth killer unless you have a plan in place.**

> - **Income taxes continue to be one your life's biggest expenses, larger than any other expense. Without a good plan, taxes will continue to hold you back.**

> - **Women typically have less in pensions and Social Security (compared to men) on which to depend.**

> - **Without a written and updated financial plan, you will continue to ask, "What do you think of", instead of having**

a system for making wise money decisions. (Decisions by consensus)

➢ As a whole, there are no good/bad products or services. It is usually that people use the wrong tool for the wrong job.

➢ Financial Plans can fail because:

   o Women may not implement their plans.

   o Women may get financial plans done by salespeople more interested in selling a product than helping them accomplish their life's goals.

   o Women or their advisors may not be committed to an ongoing plan of measurement and management and they stop working the plan.

➢ Women typically concentrate too much on perfection instead of looking at progression.

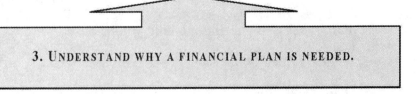

3. UNDERSTAND WHY A FINANCIAL PLAN IS NEEDED.

Notes

UNLESS YOU DO SOMETHING

BEYOND WHAT YOU HAVE ALREADY

MASTERED...

YOU WILL NEVER GROW!

CHAPTER FIVE

THE CEMENT MIXER

The Top Six Reasons People Make Bad Financial Decisions

Let us assume at this point, you now realize that you should create a solid financial plan. Let us further assume you have implemented your plan. Now, what are the obstacles you may face, what could go wrong? One of the philosophies of The Strategic Coach is that if you create a goal you should first look at all the obstacles you will encounter. By concentrating on the obstacles *first*, you will discover the answers to reaching to your goals.

Here are some of the obstacles you may encounter in your quest to develop that perfect lifestyle that you want:

1) Emotional vs. Logical decision making
2) Working Hard vs. Working Smart
3) Knowledge - *Not knowing what you do not know*
4) Knowing what you should focus on
5) Knowing your Unique Ability

6) Be aware of the impact your behavior has on your financial security

{I must give credit where credit is due. Bob Curtis who created Money Guide Pro (which, in my opinion, is one of the best online goals-based financial planning systems I have ever used. WWW.moneyguidepro.com) was kind enough to let me use this illustration for your benefit.}

In most cases, we all like to think of ourselves as logical, mechanical thinking and decision-making machines. Daily, we take in all kinds of data from the hundreds of television stations, Internet portals, newspapers, magazines, and newsletters, not to mention all the rumors, hearsay, and gossip. Then, we believe we are able to process this information into a rational conclusion or decision.

The following is an example that shows how we would all like to think of ourselves:

Most of us view ourselves as...
A Logical Thinking Machine

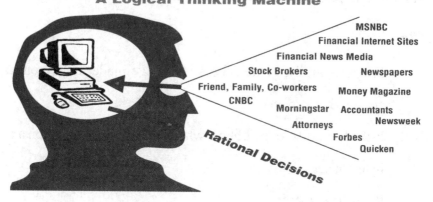

MSNBC
Financial Internet Sites
Financial News Media
Stock Brokers   Newspapers
Friend, Family, Co-workers   Money Magazine
CNBC
                Morningstar   Accountants
                                  Newsweek
                Attorneys
                         Forbes
                             Quicken

Rational Decisions

What are we really like?

What We Actually Found...
A Cement Mixer

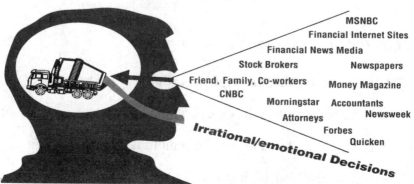

MSNBC
Financial Internet Sites
Financial News Media
Stock Brokers   Newspapers
Friend, Family, Co-workers   Money Magazine
CNBC
                Morningstar   Accountants
                                  Newsweek
                Attorneys
                         Forbes
                             Quicken

Irrational/emotional Decisions

Unfortunately it's a dirty cement mixer, with old biases, experiences, opinions, fears and aspirations.

This is what usually happens. We take in all this information and it is clogged up with experiences, biases, emotion, and confusions. To add to that, many of us are still making decisions by consensus.

Here are a few areas where this misinformation comes from:

1) Friends, family, or neighbors who have made money on a certain investment
2) Friends, family, or neighbors who may have lost money on an investment
3) Rear view mirror
4) Emotion
5) Parents

Let us take a closer look at each one:

1) **Friends, family, or neighbors who may make money**

   Have you ever had the experience where someone made a lot of money and you hear it from multiple sources? Then you believe that you are losing out and you want to get in on the action.

   a. Do you remember the stock market bubble of 1997 through 2000? Did you participate in that? Do you remember getting excited about it and wanting to get into it? Did you think it would continue to go up?

b. Do you remember the real estate bubble of 2005? Did you participate in that? Did you know someone who made a ton of money in that bubble?

c. What about the Gold Rush of 1849? How many people picked up their entire lives and moved across the country to find gold. Unfortunately, the gold rush was just like the stock market of the late nineties and the real estate bubble of 2004/2005; only the first ones in made the big money and only if they got out at the right time.

2) Friends, family members, or neighbors that lose money on an investment

How did that affect your decision-making the next time the same or a similar investment opportunity came up? How many times have you sabotaged your financial future because of your outdated knowledge? How many times have you decided not to do something because you heard that a neighbor lost money in a certain investment?

3) Rear View Mirror

This is much like your friends, family members, or a neighbor losing money, but it is **you** this time. You tried something in the past and it did not work so you figured that it would never work. Are there other people that might have the same investment that they bought at a different time and they have been successful in getting it to work? Could it be the time or the way in which you did it, or the knowledge base you had at the time? Do you base current decisions on experiences that would not be the same today?

4) Emotion

Emotion is the number one controlling factor in your financial success. Emotion will internally rule your decisions. Did you feel differently about risk the day after the attacks on 9/11? I know I did. When you watch T.V. or read the newspaper and all you read about is how bad the economy is, or about how our whole world is falling in around us, how do you feel? How does this affect your confidence? How does this affect your ability to make sound and wise money decisions? Emotion will rule your financial decisions, which, in turn, will rule your financial success, which in turn, will determine the lifestyle you will live.

I have a suggestion. Stop reading the newspaper, stop watching the news and stop absorbing the negativity of the world. Later in this book, I will teach you how you do not need this information on a daily or even weekly basis to have a successful financial future. (If Warren Buffet can admit to not having to watch the stock market, why must we be consumed by it? Warren once said he could turn off the stock market for a year and it would not affect him.) There are certain fundamental factors you do need to know about money and investments, but what you see on a daily basis is to sell the media. Having to watch over financial data is not a good way to enjoy your life.

Let me continue on the emotion factor because I feel it needs much attention. In working with so many people over the years, we have had the unfortunate experience of having clients pass away. I can tell you that when you lose a partner or a loved one there is a grieving period that I have seen last as little as one year to as long as five years, some people never fully recover. During this time, it makes the most sense to have a good wealth manager in place and a financial plan that does not have to be looked at every day. During the grieving process, I have noticed that the survivor does not always make logical or rational decisions, but rather decisions more out of emotion.

An example is a recent experience involving a new client whose husband had passed away. He had handled everything as far the financial aspect of their lives together. After meeting with the widow, my recommendation was to immediately sell the house and downsize because her husband did not leave her in a financial position to afford the house. She was against this because she had made so many memories there. While they are important memories, she had to make a choice for her own financial survival and had a very difficult time because of her emotions. How you process news and information will affect you emotionally, which in turn will affect your money decisions.

5) Parents

Your parents can have a profound influence on your decision making process. How your parents grew up can sometimes create a problem with people making sound and wise financial decisions. Many people that grew up either during The Depression *or with parents* that grew up during The Depression have certain beliefs about money. While they think their beliefs are reality, these beliefs are only their perceptions of reality.

WHAT REALITY IS TO YOU IS NOT WHAT IS NECESSARILY REAL

Some of the things your parents said stick with you and influence how wise you are with your money decisions.

To give you and example, try to fill in the blanks:

A. Money does not _____ on trees.

B. To get ahead you have to work _____.

C. Don't ever spend your _____.

D. Don't ever have a _____.

E. Always pay off your _____.

F. _____ is always a good investment.

G. The rich get richer and the _____ get _____.

H. Those that _____ lose.

I. Wait and do not make any _____decisions.

Answers:

A. Grow

B. Hard

C. Principal

D. Mortgage

E. Mortgage

F. Real Estate

G. Poor and Poorer

H. Hesitate

I. Quick

Not only are some of these false, but much of what you have heard is contradictory! **Things do not change over time, only the way you and I perceive them**.

I can tell you that when I was growing up I had no programming of false perceptions. I simply had no programming because no one ever spoke of money! I talk to friends and they tell me about their parents making comments and talking to them about these false beliefs. I am not sure which is worse, being programmed with a faulty belief system or not having one at all! If you grew up in a household that did not talk about money, then you might have gone out and created your own false beliefs from media sources, friends, relatives, neighbors, or your own perceptions from experiences.

You have this program running in your mind about how you think about and how you handle money. This program is like a giant filing cabinet. Every time you have to make a decision, your mind goes to this giant filing cabinet and searches for experiences and beliefs. Whether they are right or wrong does not matter. What matters is that, if you had the experience yourself, you will first use that as your reference point. If you have not had an experience, you try to think if you have read anything or know anyone that has had that experience that you can pull from. By not having a financial plan in place, you default to making decisions by consensus, which is illogical.

I am sure some of the experts in this area could identify better some of the reasons that you make certain money decisions. I would recommend reading anything from Anthony Robbins, T. Harv Elker (*Secrets of the Millionaire Mind*), Jack Canfield (*Chicken Soup for the Soul*), or even the golden oldie, *Think and Grow Rich* by Napoleon Hill.

These books and authors might lend more insight into why so many people sabotage their own financial futures and live a life of quiet desperation.

Working Hard vs. Working Smart

Such a simple theory and yet so many people find it difficult to master. How many hours are in the day? (I will not even print the answer to that one.) Are you really living your life to the fullest? Now, do not rationalize! Are you really experiencing everything you can and making an impact to improve others' lives? What have you done today to improve the world? Will you leave this world a better place? If not, let me ask you, are there other people that you either know, have read about, or see on TV that are living the life you would like? Are there other people that *are* making a difference in this world? Is your focus more on *yourself, your* money, and *your* security or do you have a financial plan that allows you to focus on improving *other* people's lives?

How many hours in the day does everyone have? That is right, the same as you. Then, why is it that there are other people seeing better results? Could it be that they think differently? Could it be that they work *smarter* than you do?

Charles Schwab (the original) was hired by Andrew Carnegie at the turn of the last century to run US Steel Corporation. He was paid an unheard of- one million dollars at the time. A newspaper reporter asked Mr. Schwab what he knew about steel and he said, "Not much". Then he was asked if he had ever run a steel company before. Again, he answered, "No". Then the reporter, being curious, asked how Mr. Carnegie could justify paying Mr. Schwab one million dollars if he was not an expert at steel manufacturing and sales.

Mr. Schwab's statement was classic and illustrates something about how to run your own finances with better success. He replied, "I am not paid to be an expert with steel. I am paid to get results." *(You do not receive compensation to know or educate yourself on every detail. You make money by assembling high quality teams.)*

You could say you are the hardest worker and able to work twenty hours a day and need only four hours of sleep like Donald Trump. If you did, would it really give you the lifestyle and allow you to live the life you want? To get the life you want, you have to involve other people to help you get there. ***This means working smart!***

I have met so many people that are having what I call a *financial management nervous breakdown*. They have tried to do things themselves and, after a few years, they realize that they cannot be an expert in taxes, investment, insurance, and estate planning. They have come to us in desperation, asking us to please help them get not only their financial lives on track, but also help them to have *a life*.

The ones I empathize with are the ones who continue to say "But I really do have a life." Yet, they continue to read the financial news and spend time on their computer. Working *smart* means thinking like the owner of a large business that is going to put together a team of experts that will run the company.

Knowledge- Not knowing what you do not know

Teenagers will tell you about how much they know and about how you are wrong and they are right. If you have ever had a teenager, you can relate. What is amazing is that, for many people, this attitude does not change the older they get. *We do not know what we do not know.* Have you ever heard that? Let me state it again. *We do not know what we do not know!*

Think about it for just a moment. What if you are doing your own financial management and you make a tax mistake, an investment mistake, or worse, you underinsure? If you were working with experts in these areas, could these issues be avoided, eliminated, or solved? It is funny, as we all get older, what we learn is that we really do not know as much as we thought we did when we were younger. Some people take longer to realize this than others and then they run out of time! They have spent their lives as a slave to their own limitations instead of living their life to the fullest. It not only happens with money decisions, but in other aspects of life, as well. I have found very few things in which I am really an expert. The things in which I am not an expert, I hire out. It has taken me many years to get to this humble place in my life where I realize I should only be doing certain things and I am not an expert in everything. I have found the area of wealth management so complex that even I do not profess myself as an expert in all facets. This is the reason that we outsource many of these specialties to people who devote a lifetime to certain areas of financial planning.

As of the writing of this book, I have been working in the financial services field for more than twenty years. I work an average of forty-eight weeks a year and forty hours a week. That is, one-thousand, nine hundred and twenty hours a year for the last twenty years, this is over thirty-eight thousand hours of experience. Even with all that experience, I have no qualms admitting that I am not an expert in each one of these areas. Yet, I meet people every day that tell me they are able to handle all their financial and wealth management and need no help at all! To summarize, I hope you, too, are able to admit that you are not an expert in each of these areas.

This is one of the reasons why a *good* wealth management firm will not profess to be ***all things to all people.*** They will have a team of people that they can assemble to be experts in each of the needed areas. They will not work with everyone and may have certain criteria before accepting new clients.

A talk show host once asked Bill Cosby what his key to success was. He answered, "I am not sure I could tell you the key to success, but I can tell you what the key to failure is, trying to be all things to all people." That piece of wisdom also applies to the way you approach your own finances and when you hire a wealth manager.

Knowing what your focus should be:

This is one of the most difficult things for a person to do with their finances because they are always taught to work *hard* rather than to work *smart,* which is why most people focus on the little details. Over the years, I have noticed that people have difficulty acting with vision and succumb to micromanaging.

They say things like:

➢ *"Do you think with the recent oil prices we should be shifting money to the oil sector?"*

> *"Do you think with the recent increase/decrease in interest rates we should be making some major moves?"*

> *"I see one of the managers we are using bought Home Depot and I just read a negative article about the company. Don't you think we should be contacting the manager to see what he thinks?"*

On and on... these micromanagement questions come up. Let me ask you a question. If you continue to focus on things you cannot change, what will change or improve in your life? If you focus on things you can change, what do you think will happen? You are right! You will start to see the changes because you are now focusing on things you can control.

Things you can control:

1) *Living your life in accordance to your values, (Do you have your values written out?)*

2) *Your goals (Do you have your goals written out with an action plan?)*

3) *Your budget (How much money you spend?)*

4) *Your asset allocation model (What percent you have in each asset class?)*

5) *Your plan coordination (Is your overall plan coordinated for optimal efficiency?)*

6) *The amount of current risk (Do you have your downside protected?)*

7) *Your estate and distribution planning*

8) *Your tax plan (Do you have a tax plan that is minimizing your tax expense?)*

9) *Measurement and management of progress towards your goals (Are you measuring your progress towards your goals? Do you have a system for measurement and management?)*

How interesting! If you focus on the things in your life you *can* control, do you think you will make more progress towards your ideal lifestyle? YES! Focusing on all the things you *cannot* control will only get you more of the same.

Things you CANNOT control:

1) *World Economy*

2) *Unemployment Rate*

3) *Interest Rates*

4) *Oil Prices*

5) *GNP - GROSS NATIONAL PRODUCT*

6) *Geo-Political Events*

7) *Corporate Criminals*

8) Bond Markets

9) Stock Markets

10) Mutual Fund Scandals

This list goes on and on but you get the point. Stop spending your time trying to understand how these all fit into your overall plan or how you can manipulate things to be ahead based on these events. If you are going to spend your time on anything, start with better vision. Your goals and your vision are the things you can control. You first must understand what is important about having money and what financial security means to you. We will talk more about this under goal setting.

Focus on the things you want, you will then have a foundation for creating a plan.

Summary:

➤ **Education is not the only key to financial success. Higher education does not mean that you will make logical decisions over emotional ones.**

➤ **Many forces pull and tug at you every day. Emotions can and will rule decisions. A financial coach can help** you wade through all the money decisions without the emotion.

➢ What you perceive as reality may not be reality. Your perception of certain financial decisions is based on your knowledge at the time, which may be faulty, or based on your experiences, which may be under different circumstances!

➢ Working hard is not the answer! You can work hard at your finances, but if you are making unwise money decisions, the hard work will not pay off. Working smart, together with taking wise actions, is the way to get to your goals.

➢ When someone thinks they know everything, they usually know the least.

➢ Know what you should focus on and what you can and cannot control.

Action:

➢ Make a list of all the areas of your life you can control and the ones you cannot. Start working on the ones you can control. The areas you cannot control - stop stressing about them!

➤ Focus on helping others, whether it is your family, charities or someone you do not know yet.

➤ Start thinking of all the areas of your life you would like to change or improve. Write each area down and, if money can improve it, put a $ next to it.

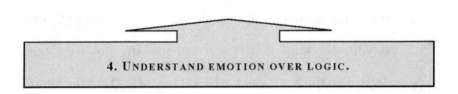

4. UNDERSTAND EMOTION OVER LOGIC.

Notes

The one asset that you spend everyday, but can

never get back!

CHAPTER SIX

STOP HERE

Stop! Take a break to think through some thoughts before you go any further! As you have found out, I am in favor of you finding a wealth manager (coach) and having that wealth manager help you achieve your life's goals. I know some of you can have all the proof in the world that the most successful people in history have found coaches to help them get to the apexes of their lives, but you still might want to do it all yourself. No matter what I say, you will still believe the media sources trying to convince everyone that they can do everything themselves. That is OK! You will still get value out of this book because you have just learned what some of your major obstacles are going to be, if you find a wealth manager (coach) or do-it- yourself. You will find the next chapters will help even if you are a do-it-yourselfer. For those of you that understand the power and speed to success you can attain by finding and hiring a coach, later chapters will help you to prepare before meeting with a financial coach (wealth manager).

At the end of this book, you will find checklists of how to find, evaluate, and manage your financial coach (wealth manager). Put your seatbelt on because there is no exit if you continue from here!

Summary:

➢ **Decide on whether you are going to go it alone or if you want a coach to help you through your journey!**

Action:

➢ **If you are going to go it alone, make a list of all the educational material you must acquire.**

➢ **Make a schedule of how much time you are going to invest in learning about all the areas of wealth management.**

➢ **Write out a list of all the software or tools that you will need to put together and operate your wealth management plan.**

➢ **Write out a budget for the cost of the educational, management, and research materials.**

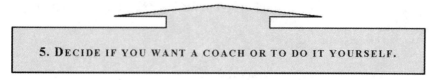

5. DECIDE IF YOU WANT A COACH OR TO DO IT YOURSELF.

THE DASH

I read of a woman who stood to speak
at the funeral of a friend.
She referred to the dates on her tombstone
from the beginning...to the end.

She noted that first came her date of birth
and spoke the following date with tears,
but she said what mattered most of all
was the dash between those years.

For that dash represents all the time
that she spent alive on earth
and now only those who loved her
know what that little line is worth.

For it matters not, how much we own,
the cars...the house...the cash.
What matters is how we live and love
and how we spend our dash.

So think about this long and hard,
are there things you'd like to change?
For you never know how much time is left
that can still be rearranged.

If we could just slow down enough
to consider what's true and real
and always try to understand
the way other people feel.

And be less quick to anger
and show appreciation more
and love the people in our lives
like we've never loved before.

If we treat each other with respect
and more often wear a smile...
remembering that this special dash
might only last a little while.

So when your eulogy is being read
with your life's actions to rehash,
would you be proud of the things they say
About how you spent your dash?

LIVE RICH & STAY WEALTHY

In the following section, I am sharing with you some stories of my clients. They have allowed me to share these stories in the hopes of perhaps sparing someone else, possibly you, from going through some of the difficult times they had to endure. Please read each one of them. I believe you will find them helpful and you may be able to relate to one or more of them. I am sure that once you read these stories you will realize just how important it is to have a plan, and a team in place!

The Story of Martha and John
Married – Children – Educated – Widowed

Martha grew up in a middle class family and her parents were both educated and believed in education. While both of her parents had college degrees they were not educated in money matters. Martha's parents were both children that went through The Great Depression and saw the problems that happened during those twelve years. They experienced serious money issues that affected their ability to make wise money decisions. Unfortunately, her parents conditioned Martha to think in the same manner. After Martha obtained her college degree, she met John. John grew up in the same environment as she did. **What is that saying about "birds of a feather?"**

John and Martha had three children together. During their marriage, John took care of all the family finances while Martha was in charge of the household and children. Martha, other than having a budget for household expenses, was unaware of what was going on. They saved and they cut corners and finally they were able to send all three of their children to college. Martha really did not know much about John's investments. She was unaware of how much insurance he had, or the income necessary to take care of them. She did not know how much they would need for retirement, nor did she and John sit down to map out a plan with values, goals, and actions. Like most people, they just wanted to get to the next day and hoped that John kept his job. When it came to insurance and investments, both John and Martha felt better trying to figure it all out on their own because they had never met someone they could trust.

*Now that you know a little bit about Martha's history, let me tell you why she was referred to me. Martha and John were doing fine and then John came down with Alzheimer's disease. John was committed to a full-time nursing care facility at an annual cost of $74,000 per year. Their total assets were $454,000 when John went into the home. He was in the home for just about three years before he passed away. At this point, Martha was left at the young age of sixty-four to try to figure out how she was going to afford the rest of her life on the remaining money of $221,000. This is the amount she had left over when she came to me about a year after John died. When I asked her what she was going through and why she was here to see me, she said, "I really feel as though much of my time is being consumed trying to learn **how** to manage my money, as opposed to, actually managing it." She went on to say that when she was not taking time to manage her money, she was worrying about it. When I asked her how she would like to live the rest of her life, she said, "I would just like to have an income that would support my lifestyle and I don't want to have to think about or worry about managing* all the details with investments, taxes, trusts and insurance". She finished up by saying, "Ken, I want the rest of my life to count and I don't think I am doing that with all the time I am spending trying to manage my affairs".

This story, while it is about one actual person, can be related to many of the women I have met over the years. Here are some of the problems that Martha not only ran into but also could have avoided if she and John had put a plan together:

1) **Women are at risk when the man has the larger pension and Social Security:**

   a. **When John went into the nursing home he had the pension income in his name**

   b. **The larger Social Security income was in his name**

      i. **This usually presents a problem to women because when the man goes into the nursing home (depending on the state you live in), the income will be used for the nursing home expense.**

      ii. **In their case, they did not hire a financial planner that specialized in these issues so they immediately made application to Medicaid and were turned down because of their assets.**

Medicaid then issued them an exclusion period, which required Martha and John to pay for the care out of their assets and income before Medicaid would kick in.

    iii. In this case, fortunately and unfortunately, John passed away before all the assets had been spent down, which would have destroyed Martha.

c. *After John passed away, they had numerous assets and investments in different names. This was very cumbersome and created additional hassles for Martha.*

d. *Martha and John had a will that named Martha as the primary beneficiary.*

    i. The problem was while John was managing his own investments he had set up more than twenty-four different accounts between banks, mutual fund companies, and discount brokerage firms.

ii. Martha had to hire an attorney to run all of his accounts (that were not listed jointly) through probate. Thankfully, she told me that she was able to get all the assets. Nine months and $7,500 in attorney fees later, she finally had all the assets in her name.

She told me that she felt ignorant that she had let John handle all of this and she never really knew where it all was or if it was right. She still had all twenty-four of these accounts and, in addition, IRAs, annuities, and life insurance that she still had not yet finished the claim. She also said that she still had to change the deeds to the house, the credit cards, and all the other titles like automobiles, insurance, etc.

OUR PLAN

*Our first step together was to develop a plan that would allow us to see where she would be if she did not make **any** changes. The challenges were many.*

Here is a small list of what was recommended:

1) *Meet with an attorney to set up a revocable living trust and transfer all the assets into this trust so that when she passed away her children would not have to go through probate.*

2) Have the attorney create ancillary documents:

    a. Pour Over Will

    b. Health Care Surrogate

    c. Durable Power of Attorney

    d. Living Will

3) Change her investment structure. John managed everything based on emotion and trying to predict the markets. Martha's concern was to have a steady income and to be stress free about the risk.

4) Develop a budget based on her income. John had a haphazard budget that he never shared with her. This budget needed to account for whether she felt it was important to leave something to her children after her death or if she felt it more important to live to her fullest financial potential. She chose the latter.

5) Obtain a long-term care insurance policy, to assure her independence. She found out later that the home they chose for John was based on what they could afford. After he was there, she told me about the lack of care, the unsanitary conditions, and the overall low quality of care. She told me that if that ever happened to her, she would really want the option to choose whether she would go in a home or have in-home care. If she were to go into a home, she wanted to

not only choose the home, but also have a private room as opposed to a semi-private room as John had.

The overall goal was to allow her to spend more time with her children and grandchildren without having to worry about all the money issues. With many couples today, one of the spouses takes care of the finances and it is usually the male. This management style leaves the female out in the cold. If you are married, here is a list of questions you should ask your spouse so that you are not in the dark:

> **What is the amount of money you would need if you lost your spouse?**
>
> > *1) Monthly*
> >
> > *2) Annually*
> >
> > *3) What would your budget be?*
>
> **What is the amount of liquid assets you have in your name?**
>
> **What have your investment returns been the last one, three and five years?**
>
> **What is your investment risk? (Quantify on a scale of one-ten) Ten is the riskiest.**
>
> **How much life insurance do you need on your partner?**
>
> **How much life insurance do you have now? What is the cost and will it run out at any period? If your husband has**

group insurance through his employer, will that end when he retires? Will it be reduced?

➢ Are all the accounts titled in your trust name, JTWROS (Joint Trust with Rights of Survivorship), or some title that will assure passing to you without probate?

➢ Are you named as the beneficiary of your husband's retirement plan, annuity, or life insurance? Do you have a copy of the beneficiary form on hand? (This goes back to a case where the IRS taxed a woman because the bank could not produce the beneficiary form and the account holder did not have one either, so the life expectancy was zero. (IRA))

➢ Do you have advance directives, last wills, durable power of attorneys, and health care surrogates naming you for your husband?

➢ What is you total debt? What would it take to make those payments if your spouse died?

This is only a short list but identifies some of the most important issues. I think you will be able to determine how well you know your situation by answering these questions.

Summary:

➤ Education is not the only key to financial success!

➤ What your parents have taught you can influence your money decisions.

➤ It is all right to have one spouse handle the bookkeeping, but do not let one spouse handle all the money decisions. Both parties are involved and at risk so, like a business partnership, have regular meetings. (Couples have told me that the only time they had financial business meetings that were constructive and did not end in arguments is when they came in to meet with me.)

➤ Do not wait to protect your assets.

➤ Have a system for making wise money decisions so if one spouse dies the survivor will already be in that system.

➤ Consolidate financial information- Too many financial statements only make management harder.

➤ Make sure that each person has credit in their own name.

➤ Have a written financial plan in place and have it updated each year.

The Story of Joan

Single – Educated

Joan came to us in her late sixties and had done all of her own wealth management until she was diagnosed with cancer. With sickness, she started to realize that she had spent an awful amount of time trying to learn and keep up on all the tax rules, investment strategies, watching the stock market and insurance costs. Joan had never been married, but had been an executive all her life. She was an accountant for a large company that paid her very well. She had been through college and, just like Martha, had grown up in a family where her parents conditioned much of her monetary thinking.

*I asked her why she had done all of her own money management. She said it was because she felt as though she was educated and since she was an accountant she should know all there is to know about the management of money. What really keyed me in was when she said she had to work **hard** to get everything she had. The conversation was very interesting in that I kept hearing about how she should know all these things and how she had to manage her own affairs. She kept saying that the harder she worked the better the results would be. I asked her where this all came from and she told me that her father was a blue-collar worker and instilled a hard work ethic in her. I asked her what that meant. She said that she felt that the* *harder you work at something the better off you will be. I asked her if her father told her to **work hard** or to **work smart**. She said with a smirk on her face, "He always told me to work hard." "I can hear him saying over and over again", Go to college, work hard and you will have anything you want." "Now I don't know how true that really is," she said.*

I asked Joan why she spent so many years following this philosophy. She said that she could now see why it took her developing cancer to realize that we all have such a short time and that there were more important things to do with her time. I then asked what she really wanted to do with her time. Joan said that she wanted to relax a little, since she realized that she had a short time. She wanted someone she could trust so she could concentrate on the more important things in life. I asked Joan what she thought the more important things in her life were and she actually surprised me. I thought with her sickness she would have said, just to have some time with friends and family. She did say that, but it was lower on the list. She told me she wanted the following:

1) ***Bike across the U.S. to raise money for cancer awareness***

2) ***Volunteer time at the local Women's Resource Center***

3) ***Go to three Women's Professional Golf Tournaments***

4) ***Go to the Wimbledon tennis match every year***

5) *See the Grand Canyon and take a friend that she had met during her cancer treatments*

6) *Take the summer and baby-sit for her niece and nephew's children.*

I was impressed. I told her that I understood why she was in my office. When people are diagnosed like this, I have seen some of them just start spending with no regard for the fact that they may get better, but then they will be out of money. I told her it was very important that we put priorities on these goals and we set them up so they could be accelerated if the sickness got worse. She had some things that she wanted to do before she passed away that would leave an impact on the world, more so than her sitting behind her computer to make stock trades.

The most rewarding part of my mission is to see the success of a person once they have a plan that will allow them to accomplish their goals. In Joan's case, once we input her goals and put dollar amounts on them it was interesting to see if she would be able to accomplish all of her goals.

I once heard a late night talk show host ask George Burns what his secret to a long life was and he said, "To have goals to accomplish into the future". He then said he had shows scheduled out for the next three years and he was ninety-seven years young at the time.

OUR PLAN

I asked Joan when she wanted to accomplish her goals. She said, "As soon as possible". Therefore, we scheduled the longest goal out for three years. One of her main concerns was, if she were to pass away, she wanted to make sure that her assets would be left to a charity that would fund cancer research. Here is a short list of some of the changes we made in her plan:

1) **We changed the investment portfolio to fit an income strategy to help fund her goals with the extra cash flow.**

2) **We created a Family Foundation- This is a device, which allows part of her assets to be placed into a trust, and she will receive a tax deduction on the transfer. While she is alive, she will operate the Foundation, which will give a certain amount to her charities each year. The Foundation will also pay her an income, which will allow her to accomplish some of her goals. Her desire was that after she passes away, she wants the Foundation to continue, so we named her niece and nephew as the next in line to run it. They will then receive an income to run it and will be required to contribute a certain amount from the Foundation to her cancer research charity.**

3) *Even though she was an accountant for a large company, she was never schooled on tax management. We set up strategies to reduce the amount of income tax she was paying on her investment income, which meant we could invest with less risk since she now enjoyed a higher after-tax return.*

This is a short list, but it gives you an idea of what some of your possibilities could be. One other part of this plan should be noted.

Joan wanted to have someone take over the financial management of her money. If you decide you are going to find a financial coach, then you have to make sure that they are going to hold you accountable. Let me explain. If you hire a personal trainer, you tell them the results you want and then they put you on a diet and/or a physical training schedule. If you gain weight and do not get the results, it is probably because you ate more than the plan allowed or did not work out as much as the plan required.

It is not much different when it comes to a financial plan. Over the years, I have seen examples where people would hire a wealth manager (coach) and they complained because they did not get the outcome that they wanted. The wealth manager (coach) had outlined what was needed and the client would do just the opposite and then blame the wealth manager (coach) for not achieving their goals. A long time ago, I figured out that in a coaching type of relationship, the client would hold the wealth manager (coach) accountable for doing what they were supposed to do, but the wealth manager (coach) rarely holds the client accountable for their actions. However, if the wealth manager (coach) is going to get their client to achieve their goals they must also start to hold their client accountable.

I told Joan that we would help her, as long as she was committed to results and willing to be held accountable for her actions. At the beginning of the relationship, she agreed. Then, it came to starting the plan to reaching her goals. One of our accountability techniques is to write down our clients' goals, attach the dollars needed and then the dates desired. Then take the plan and work backwards, putting together a financial plan to get them to their goals. The client has to participate because, in most cases, there are action tasks that they must do in order to reach these goals.

If your goal is to take a vacation with your family for a month on a cruise ship around the world, the wealth manager (coach) needs to determine the best way to financially get you there. You need to research the cruise ships, get a travel agent, and start making your plans. In this case, like so many, I advised Joan that she needed to start gathering the information on how she would make this bike trip, travel to the Grand Canyon and go to the golf and tennis tournaments. The plan was for her to do all the research over the next few months.

We met again after a few months to review her financial plan and to see the progress she made on her goals. Unfortunately, she made no progress. She said that she thought about it after she made these plans, but then she just got too busy. At this point, **Coach Ken** had to step in, and with loving care, explain that she had the opportunity to live these goals and dreams and we had set up her finances to make it happen. We could not make it happen for her if she was not committed. I explained that she had promised to work on these goals and while she would hold us accountable for keeping her money on track, we would hold her accountable for her goals participation. I asked her what she would have done if we had not followed through with anything we said we would do, and she said, "I would have been really upset with you." I then responded, "I hope you understand we have a mutually beneficial relationship and we can only keep clients that hold up their end of the bargain." Then she said, startled, "You would fire me?" I said, "Yes, I would. I would not enjoy it because I like you, but if you don't follow through with your goals then it would be the best for both of us to part ways."

With that in mind, we set up a new schedule for her to do the research on reaching her goals. I called her a month later and she had all of her goals researched, put on her calendar and she *was incredibly excited about them. It is amazing what you can accomplish once you have a written plan with dates, amounts and an action plan.*

**A goal without
an amount, a date and an action plan
is only an empty wish.**

Summary:

> Education is not the only key to financial success!

> Do not wait to start enjoying your life; it could be over in a second.

> Let money work for you as a tool and do not get bogged down with the time it takes to manage your wealth.

> Work smart, not hard!

> Have compelling and inspirational goals. Think about not only improving your life but what could you do to improve or help someone else.

> Put together a written financial blueprint and have it updated annually.

> Have a system to manage your wealth automatically so you do not have to do all the heavy lifting.

> Do not wait to implement your plan – you do not have a promise of tomorrow!

The Story of Melinda

Divorced – Remarried – Children

Melinda, who is now a client, came to us in her mid sixties after being married for twenty plus years and she had now remarried. She had three children from her first marriage and her new husband had three children as well.

Cases like Melinda's are even more complex. It is hard enough to keep a good marriage in today's environment. Add in children and it is even harder. Add in children from previous marriages and it can make life more stressful. Here is what Melinda's financial situation looked like when she first contacted me:

> ➢ *When she was divorced, she got the house, some investment assets, and some of the retirement plans. The house at the time of the divorce was only worth $150,000. It was now worth over $600,000. One of those lucky real estate growth stories from Florida!*

> ➢ *Her house was originally put into her name by the divorce court, but after twenty plus years of marriage to the new husband (we will just call him Bill for the sake of privacy), she changed the house and put the house into joint tenancy. This means that they went to the county clerk's office and filed a new deed with both names.*

> She had a will and it stated that upon her death her house would go to Bill. However, if Bill died first, she wanted her house to go to her children. Bill, by the way, had the same type of will.

> Her other assets were mixed between mutual funds, variable annuities, life insurance and stock brokerage accounts.

> She partly managed these investments on her own and with Bill. Bill usually made the final decision, but they had a slew of stock brokers, insurance salespeople and bank sales people.

She really had never met with a comprehensive wealth manager. To complicate matters, Bill did not want to meet with a wealth manager, as he was very independent and said it was a **waste of time**. He told Melinda, "Everything is working fine, why worry about it?"

Melinda said that she was concerned for a few reasons. These were her main concerns:

1) If something happened to Bill, she wanted to make sure that her assets would remain hers and would not pass to Bill's kids since she believed that she would need them to live on.

2) *Bill might not really know what he was doing as she felt as though their finances were all over the place. She said her financial plan seemed unorganized and not efficient.*

3) *If Bill died first, would her affairs be messy?*

4) *If she or Bill became ill, would they go bankrupt?*

5) *If something happened to her, would her assets from the divorce go to her children? She also did not want to leave Bill high and dry to support himself on his own.*

The last goal she had was one that I also hear repeatedly from women, e.g. to reduce the amount of time their partner spends on financial management. She was very upset with Bill because they had plans to travel and do things in retirement. As she said, "The only thing she did in retirement was to look at the back of his head as he worked on the computer checking on their investments, doing their taxes and all the other various financial tasks." She was sick of it and wanted some quality time with him.

These concerns are very common when we meet with second marriage clients who have children. At the beginning of the relationship, there is more emphasis and emotional attachment to the children of the first marriage. I have seen that as time goes on and the relationship builds, there becomes a balance and then, in some cases, even an overweighting to leaving assets to the new spouse.

OUR PLAN

In Melinda's case, she had pretty much the full meal deal. She had issues with risk, investments, insurance, asset distribution, protection and financial management time. Let us start with some of the basics so you can see that she actually had hope but it would not be easy with Bill at the helm.

One of the first hurdles that she had to overcome was to get Bill to agree to start helping her. In second marriages, the goal is to leave money under a fair arrangement, but I have seen one common problem: The trust design or the set up of the will.

These documents may not be designed with the second generation in mind and almost never with the third generation in mind. She now had to talk to Bill and get him to, at least agree, that if she decided to split the finances he would sign over assets to her. She was very nervous about this and she later told me it was one of the hardest things she ever had to do. I asked her how she gathered the courage to do it. She said she had a friend that had a similar situation and she had passed away. Not long afterwards, the husband passed away. All of her assets, which should have gone to her children, went to his children. Melinda said she thought about the hard time her children had with her divorce and she could not imagine that all of her assets would go to Bill's children. She really liked Bill's children, but the assets belonged to **her** children, she said. When she thought about the fact that if she did nothing this may happen, she found the courage to talk with him. When I asked how it went, she said that they started with an argument and he was mad at her for starting this whole ordeal. It ended up, however, that he really saw how concerned she was. She also asked him how he would feel if he died first, then she died and all of his assets went to her children. She told me that got his attention. Bill told her that he thought it ought to be fair.

The result was that he was still not ready to meet with me, but he would look at the plan that we created. If it were fair and to his liking, he would sign off on it. In this situation, I recommended that she split the assets into two parts:

One part that she could hire out for the wealth management and the second part that he could manage on his own. The main reason for this is that, in many cases, men, in all their overconfidence, ruin the financial future of the woman. If the woman has the longer life expectancy and will be required to live for ten years or longer than the man does, they need the financial resources to do so.

Here is a shortened version of a very complex plan:

1) We set up a multi-generational trust (MGT). This will allow her assets, including the house, to be put into this trust.

Upon her death, Bill would get an income from the trust and could take out principal withdrawals for Health, Education, Maintenance, and/or Support (HEMS). Upon Bill's death, the assets would stay in the trust, but the trust would split into three separate shares, one for each of her children. Each child could then take the income and principal withdrawals for HEMS. If one of her children were to die, become disabled, divorced, or get sued, the assets would be in the trust and would be protected. (Depending on the state, the beneficiary may or may not be protected from claims of creditors.) If one of her children were to die, the trust would absolutely assure that the money would go to her grandchildren, not to the daughter-in-law or son-in-law. We had to change the deed to the house, the beneficiary on the life insurance policy, her annuities, and her IRAs. We also had to change the titles of her investment accounts.

2) *One of her main concerns was to be sure that if something happened to Bill she would have enough money to survive. We put together a budget, as if Bill had passed away. We then set up the structure of her investments so that there would be minimal risk and so that the portfolio could be easily converted to income, if the unfortunate event happened.*

3) *We looked at the financial plan and decided that if Bill did get sick it would cripple her financially. Unfortunately, Bill did not agree with the recommendation to buy insurance to protect her. He thought that insurance was a **rip-off**, as he put it. This was quite unfortunate so we had to make a contingency plan that, if he did get sick, we would have to look at aggressive asset protection strategies to make sure she would not go broke.*

4) *Bill had not done a bad job of investing the money, but he had accounts all over the place. Once we split the assets, we consolidated all the assets into a data aggregator. This allowed us both to see all the current assets on one page. (You can learn more about this by going to www.emoney.com)*

5) *The last part of her goal was to create a lifestyle that was more enjoyable than watching the back of Bill's head at the computer. This was the hardest task to accomplish. The way we approached this was to have Bill agree that he would continue to watch over his money, as that is what made him comfortable, but he agreed that he would also participate in her travel plans.*

Three years after working on Melinda's plan, Bill called my office to schedule an appointment. Bill wanted to meet with me, personally, without Melinda. When we met, I was fearful that he was meeting with me to give me some bad news about Melinda's health. He started by telling me he wanted to meet with me alone because he really didn't want Melinda to hear **that she was right**! He told me that he was frustrated that Melinda was getting the same returns on her investments as he was, and he was spending all this time trying to do it on his own. He spoke about all the trips they were taking. He felt like every time they went somewhere, he could not enjoy himself. On one trip, he said he had to check in on his stocks and found himself watching CNBC in the hotel. He said they went on the trip with some friends and, in their discussion, their friends said, "Bill isn't really retired. He is tied to the computer everyday." Then he told me about their cruise. He ended up on the Internet at thirty bucks an hour just so he could make his trades. He told me he had seen the other side of investing and that Melinda was really enjoying herself. He wanted that same set up.

This is not the first time this has happened. If you have a partner or husband that is like Bill, stay strong. Make sure you stand up for yourself. You have to make sure that you can take care of yourself. While many men do a good job of managing the money, what happens if they die first, you get divorced or they become disabled? You owe *it to yourself to get a grasp on your money and, if your partner does not want to participate, look at it like a hobby. If you want to take up a new hobby and your spouse does not want to participate, what would you do? I am sure, like most women today; you would take up the new hobby without him. The key in these situations is to get the result in a harmonious and emotionally acceptable way between the two of you.*

Summary:

> Education is not the only key to financial success!

> Do not let your spouse hold you back from protecting your own financial future! If your husband is not a willing participate, do it yourself!

> If you want to assure your assets go to your intended heirs make sure your estate and distribution plan is correct.

> Your stepchildren or even your own children may be the nicest people in the world, but remember two things: First, they might have spouses and, second, money changes people!

> Have a written financial blueprint and have it updated annually. Last year's plan is already outdated. Look at how many changes happen in just the tax code each year.

➤ Do not make an uneducated statement about insurance such as Bill did. Insurance is only a tool that some should use and others should avoid, but only after a careful risk analysis is done.

The Story of Evelyn

Widowed – Business Owner

Every few years I run into someone who absolutely stuns me. Evelyn is one of those people. She is a woman that I sincerely admire. She was married for over thirty years before her husband passed away. Evelyn and her husband were very successful business owners.

When Evelyn first came to see me, I was very interested in her history. I asked her how they got started in business. She said that she and her husband came from similar backgrounds. Her father-in-law ran a successful business, and so did her parents. She told me that they had a great lifestyle and were able to travel the world. They were involved in various charities and spent a lot of time bringing up their children. She was still very involved with her children and grandchildren. She also said that a majority of her time was away from the business.

Over the years, I have seen many people let their businesses run their lives. I also have seen people let their money management run their lives. I was interested in finding out how she and her husband were able to set themselves apart from the other ninety-eight percent of people. She told me that she was very lucky in that both of their parents taught them about the value of bringing expert teams of people together to get the results. She went on to tell me about their business. They had a Chief Executive Officer (CEO), Chief Operating Officer (COO), and a Chief Financial Officer (CFO). When it came to taxes, legal services and investments, they outsourced. In other words, they hired the best expertise they could find. She mentioned that long before they started their business they decided that their business was to be only a small part of their life. It would be the part that would give them money that they could use as the tool to accomplish other things in life. In order for this to happen, the business had to be able to run on its own. They would have to put together a good team. When we started talking about her personal wealth management, she and her husband used the same philosophy as they did in their business. They hired a comprehensive wealth manager, much like their CEO. It was his job to help them formulate their personal visions of what they wanted life to look like and then develop a plan that would meet that vision.

Evelyn told me a little about their relationship with their wealth manager. He was held accountable to their expectations, but he demanded a lot of them too. He was to make sure that they stayed on track to develop the vision for their lives. At this point I asked, "Why are you here, it sounds like he is doing a great job?" She said he did a great job, but unfortunately, he had passed away. He was a sole practitioner and a large company bought out his practice. She had met with the new person assigned to her and he was more concerned with selling products than helping her reach her goals. "Since you have been with such a fantastic wealth manager, you probably know what is next, right?" Evelyn answered, "I sure do. Here are all my financial papers." It was truly a magical sight. She had brought her tax returns, her insurance policies, her investment statements, and her trust. She even brought her goals, listed with dollar amounts and prioritized! I asked her if this is how she worked with her last wealth manager. She told me that is what he expected and they went through it like clockwork every year. Her last wealth manager had really done a great job. Her plan was right on track and all we had to do is pick up where he left off.

As I said, once every few years, I come across someone who really has his/her financial life under control. Evelyn is a perfect example. She spent time where she felt it was important and would leave an impact on others. She felt better having experts handle her wealth management.

Summary:

- ➤ **Education is not the only key to financial success!**
- ➤ **Just because you own a business does not make you an expert at wealth management!**

- ➢ Focus on what is most important to you and let experts handle all the other details in your life!
- ➢ You can accomplish more in life with partnerships than you can all on your own!

Smart People

LEARN THROUGH THEIR OWN EXPERIENCES...

Wise People

LEARN THROUGH THE EXPERIENCE OF OTHERS.

-Kenneth Himmler, Sr.

By now, you have heard about different women from different situations, all in need of some financial direction. You may have some of the same issues as these women, and then again, you may have a very different situation. In either case, the point is that you can see that life can be complex and confusing. I hope you can appreciate the trials these women have had to endure and learn from them. Managing your financial matters can be a stressful and complicated process. I hope that you can truly understand the importance of finding the right team of people to help you reach your goals!

VALUE YOUR LOVED ONES,

APPRECIATE THEM FOR WHO THEY ARE.

VALUE YOUR DREAMS,

HOLD ONTO THEM, FOR THEY WILL CARRY YOU

WHEN YOU FEEL WEAK.

VALUE YOUR IDEAS,

FOR THEY WILL TAKE YOU PLACES THAT WERE

ONCE ONLY IN YOUR MIND.

ABOVE ALL ELSE...

VALUE YOURSELF,

FOR YOU ARE SPECIAL AND UNIQUE IN YOUR

OWN BEAUTIFUL WAY.

Julie Berloni

CHAPTER SEVEN

YOUR VALUES

I am now going to throw you off the mainstream and into a completely new way of thinking! Have you ever had to make a financial decision and afterwards you were unsure if you made the right one? Sometimes, you simply cannot make the decision because you really do not know what is right. This is because there is the lack of a business plan for MW, Inc. *In simple terms, you do not have a current and valid financial plan!*

We are now going to walk through, systematically, creating a **strategic objective** for your MW, Inc. We start with your list of values. How do we start discovering your list of **values**? Ask the *right* questions in the *right* way! Next, we are going to create your *value steps*!

(The credit for this concept of a values-based system goes to Bill Bachrach, who developed the values-based financial planning system. I recommend that you read Bill's book titled "Values Based Financial Planning." The web site is www. bachrachvbfp.com.)

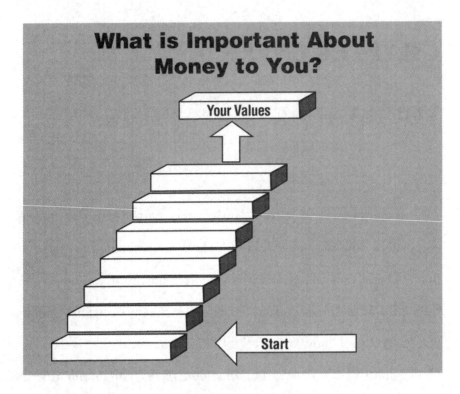

You don't need to have this exact form. You can simply take out a piece of paper and write. To help you understand how to do this correctly let me explain a little further.

You have to decide on your values. Just how important is money to you? Only you will be able to answer this question, there is no right or wrong answer!

What is important about money to you? When you have the first answer to that question, write it in. Then ask yourself, what is important about that to me. As an example, if I answered, **"security"** in the first step, I would ask myself, "What is important about security to me?" I may answer, **"Freedom."** If security is most important, what would I get if I had a feeling or knew I was secure? I would **feel free**. If I felt freedom, what would be important about that to me? If I felt freedom, I would not worry as much and would not have as much stress. What is important about not having stress or worry? If I had no stress or worry, I could use my time better, instead of worrying about money. What is important about being able to use my time wisely? If I used my time wisely, I could spend more time with my children, my family and even have more time to myself that I could enjoy. What is important about spending time with my children (without worry or stress about money), my family, and me? Then the time I spend, I could enjoy more and I could share more of myself. I could teach things to my children and grandchildren and I could be more help to my children, my family, and my community. What is important about being helpful to my children, my family, and my community without having to worry or stress about money because I have financial freedom and security? Then, I would feel as though I am living life to its fullest potential and I would feel as though I am reaching my purpose in life.

Here is an example of a client's values ladder:

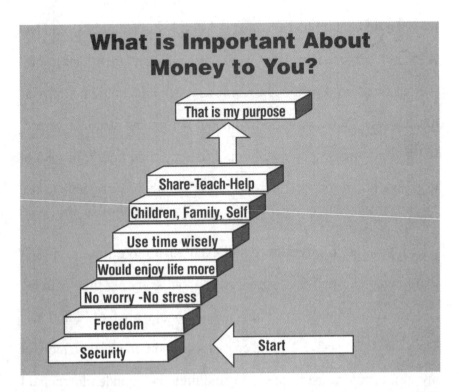

What is Important About Money to You?

That is my purpose

Share-Teach-Help

Children, Family, Self

Use time wisely

Would enjoy life more

No worry -No stress

Freedom

Security

Start

You need to keep going up the steps until you can answer this question. Is there anything more important about _____ (the top level) to you? If your answer is no, then you have your list of values in order.

Now that you have your list, understand that anytime you make a major financial decision or set a goal you should always consult with your values first. If you are married, you each need to do a separate value step. You should also go through this exercise once a year to review and discuss changes in your life as you grow mentally and financially.

Summary:

➤ Unless you know what drives your internal motivation you will continue to make emotional - financial decisions and not really know if you made the right ones - until it is either a success or a failure.

Actions:

➤ Write out a list of what is most important to you in the ladder format.

➤ Use the values to check your goals to make sure your goals are in line with what is important to you.

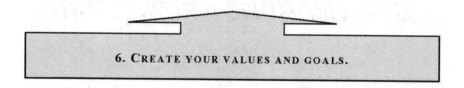

6. CREATE YOUR VALUES AND GOALS.

Goals are only wishes until

they are written

with deadline dates, dollar

amounts, and action plans

to attain them!

—Kenneth Himmler, Sr.

CHAPTER EIGHT

YOUR GOALS

What is most important about money – to you?

You can go to the bookstore and pick up hundreds of books about goals and goal setting. I think I have read about half of them. There are some good ones out there. When it comes to setting goals within a system, I have to give the credit to the Strategic Coach and the Bill Bachrach system. I am going to share a new way of thinking about your goals and how to achieve them. A goal without a date of achievement, a dollar amount, the results expected, and a written plan to get there, is only an empty wish.

Goal Setting Steps:

If you are married, then go to the next section, as you will have more steps.

Single or married women (if you handle your own finances)

1) Creative – non-limiting goal setting (Add as much as you can, without limitation, as to what you think may be possible. What

you think possible is limited right now by your perception of your capability, which may not be reality).

2) Cross check with your values

3) Prioritize

Married Women (if you manage your finances jointly)

1) Creative – non-limiting goal setting (Add as much as you can, without limitation, as to what you think may be possible. What you think is possible is limited right now by your perception of your capability, which may not be reality).

2) Cross check with your values

3) Your partner cross checks with their values

4) Create one list of goals that you jointly agree upon

5) Prioritize the joint goals

Here is an empty goal sheet that you can fill out, but I would suggest that you create your own. If you see a wealth manager (coach), I recommend you take a copy to leave with them and then keep one for yourself. You should also renew this sheet once a year, at a minimum.

Priority	Goal Name	Cost	Date	Does it match your values?

Continue with more rows if you have BIG goals.

THE BIGGER, THE BETTER!

Here is a goals sheet completed by a client:

Description of your goal	Dollar cost of goal	Target date of goal	Is goal a want or a need? (W or N)	What it the emotional benefit to you?	Does this goal meet your values?
New Car	40k	12/2008	W	Happiness	?
Debt Free	100k	06/2010	N	Less Stress	Yes
Vacation	10k	Every Year	W	Enjoyment Entertain	Yes
Hurricane Shutters	95K	09/2006	N	Safety	Yes
Medical Cost Protection	50k/Yr	Every Year	N	Security	Yes
Alice and Bob Service	6K	Every Year	W	Free Time	Yes
Gifts to Kids	5K	Every Year	W	Parental	Yes

Earlier, I said in **Step 1,** to do a creative goal setting session in which you would not be limited. The important step to creating a compelling goal list is to lose your limiting beliefs. These limiting beliefs come from many places. Some experts say by the time you are eighteen years old you are told *NO* more than forty thousand times! We are all told to live in a realistic world. What is realistic? Is this based on your perception of reality? What if Edison listened to reality on the 9,999th time the light bulb failed? It was the 10,000th time that it worked. In the mid-1800's, the statement was made that there was no use investing in anymore inventions because anything that would be useful had already been invented. In the 1950's, if you said that you could talk to your car and it would produce a map and lead you to your location, they would have thought you were nuts!

<u>**The only limit on your goals is what you believe**</u>

<u>**you can achieve and, more importantly, what you are willing to**</u>

<u>**do to achieve them!**</u>

You want to write down realistic goals that you can control and achieve. Let me give you another example. If you wrote down that you want to travel around the world by working for a cruise line and you have three children in school, this is an empty wish, unless the cruise ship has an onboard school.

You could, however, say that you want to create a financial situation that once your children are off to college (assuming you want to pay for it) you will get a job with the cruise lines teaching ballroom dancing so you can get paid for your cruises and travel. If you are having a hard time thinking of some of the potential goals, here is a list of some of the most basic and some that may inspire you to think bigger than ever before. Some of these will require money to accomplish. Others will require time and commitment and, in many cases, free time requires money.

Please write down all the goals you want on your goals sheet.

Basic examples:

1) Do not run out of money before I run out of life
2) Make sure that my children are taken care of if something happens to me or, if married, both of us
3) Be able to retire before I die
4) Make sure my assets are protected in the event that I am sued
5) Make sure I have continual income in the event that I get hurt or sick and cannot work any longer
6) Make sure I can survive if I lost my job (if married, if spouse lost job)
7) Make sure I have a safe source of transportation

8) Make sure I have the right health insurance protection in the event that I, one of my children or spouse get sick

9) Have an emergency fund

The "I want more out of life goals."

Travel:

1) Go and see a live volcano in Hawaii and then, if physically able, go skiing afterwards

2) Go to the top of Mount Halleakela to see the sunrise in Maui

3) Take the mule ride down the cliffs of the Grand Canyon

4) Go to see the whales in Vancouver

5) Visit three new ski resorts each winter

6) Spend the holidays in a small European village

7) Take a cruise down the Rhine River in Europe

8) Stay in a medieval castle in Germany

9) See the Eiffel Tower

10) Stay in a luxury hotel in Las Vegas

11) Follow the seasons by owning or renting a house in the north for the summer and the south for the winter

12) Go see the "Running of the Bulls" in Spain

13) Go to Brazil for Carnival

14) Go to New Orleans for Mardi Gras

15) Go to the Rose Bowl for the Rose Parade

16) Go to South Beach, Miami, and find the best shopping and restaurants

17) Take the American – Oriental Express train across the Canadian Rockies

18) Go to Niagara Falls

19) Go to the art shows in Palm Springs

20) Hike the Appalachian Trail

21) Go on the famous 600-mile antique trail through the Appalachian Mountain towns

22) Go on an airboat ride in the everglades

23) Go to Montana and watch the Buffalo roam

24) Go on an African safari

25) Go to the Mayan temples in Mexico

26) Go to the rain forests of Costa Rica

27) Sample Italian culture and cuisine by renting a Tuscan villa

Sports:

1) Go to the Stanley Cup Finals

2) Go to the Super Bowl

3) Go to the World Series

4) Attend a major golfing event

    a. Play golf at Pebble Beach

    b. Play golf at St. Andrews in Scotland

    c.   Get golf lessons

5) Go to the Kentucky Derby every year

6) Go to the Daytona 500

7) Buy a sports car, join a sports car club, and travel across the country

8) Attend dog shows

Health:

1) Lose weight – hire a trainer

2) Get a makeover

3) Get massages weekly

4) Go to a hot springs resort and spend a week getting pampered

5) Join a golf or tennis club

6) Go to see a chiropractor monthly

Spiritual:

1) Volunteer at church

2) Visit the Holy Land

Personal:

1) Join toastmasters and make a speech in front of a crowd

2) Learn self-defense (Karate-Tae Kwon Do)

3) Join an acting class

4) Learn ballroom dancing

5) Get a college degree

6) Take an adult education class

7) Learn how to use computer better (not so that you can spend more time managing your money!)

Charity:

1) Give money or volunteer time to:

        A. Women's Breast Cancer Foundation

        B. Battered Women's Center

        C. Women's Resource Center

        D. Nature Conservatory

        E. Save the whales

        F. Animal Cruelty

2) Volunteer at the local school

3) Join a Rotary or a Kiwanis club

4) Join my local women's community group

Tangible:

1) New Automobile

2) An RV to travel across country

3) A recreational boat

4) A vacation house in my favorite spot

Chore delegation:

1) A house cleaner

2) A cleaning person

3) A handyman/woman

4) A pool person

5) A lawn care person

Gifts:

1) Anonymous gift to someone I know that really needs the help

2) A gift to my children, maybe to help them with their first home

3) A gift to my grandchildren to help them through college

4) A gift to my spouse or partner each year to show my appreciation

5) A gift to my parents to show my appreciation for putting up with me all those years

Family Time:

1) Time to spend with my children, grandchildren, or partner

2) Volunteer to baby-sit for my children

3) Time to visit each child or grandchild in different parts of the country

4) A family reunion once a year

Distribution:

1) Set up my plan so that my children will have a certain amount or an annual income after I pass

2) A certain amount to leave to my church or charity

3) Assurance that my spouse or partner will be financially secure and able to maintain the same lifestyle that we now enjoy

Here is an assortment of other goals that might get your creative juices going:

Visit all four Grand Slam Tennis matches, The Indy 500, The NBA Championships, The Final 4, The Olympics, The Boston Marathon, and The Tour de France. If you enjoy golf, how would you like to play at: Saw Grass, Inverness, Pebble Beach, Augusta National, Oakmont, and Princeville in Kauai? How close would you like to be to your children, grandchildren, parents, brothers, sisters, aunts, uncles, cousins, nieces, and nephews? Would you like to learn to play a musical instrument? Would you like to learn to act in a play? Would you like to give money or belong to your local orchestra, drama club, and/or playhouse? Would you like to sponsor young musicians or actors? Would you like to learn to fly a plane, a helicopter, a hang glider, or an ultra-light? Would you like to learn how to jump out of a perfectly good airplane – skydiving? Would you like to learn to speak another language? Would you like to learn self-defense or even get your black belt? Would you like to travel to see the Panama Canal? You could travel to the Great Barrier Reef or the Pyramids in Egypt.

Lifestyle and Productivity

Lastly, get a job doing something you really want to do, instead of *having* to do something for the money. If you are already retired, consider a job doing something you always wanted to do but never could because you had to have a job that supported your lifestyle. I like this goal the best. Have you ever run into someone that you can tell they just love what they do? I usually meet many of these people in the travel industry.

Imagine that you are so financially set that you can choose the job you want

because it fits your U.A. (Unique Ability). You will know you have this job

when you cannot wait to get to work every day.

I hope that by now you have a compelling list of goals. Unfortunately, most people will read this and say, yeah, I will get back to this chapter and write my goals down later. Do not do this! Stop right now and start writing your goals. If you do not have a list, it is probably because you have procrastinated in the past. If you do not start now, you will probably go through the normal stages of retirement that most other women will be subjected to. Without a comprehensive list of goals and an action plan to get to these goals, you may fall into the common retirement trap.

Here is what I have observed with most people that retire:

Stage One: Retirement Planning

During this stage, people start to plan for having enough money for retirement. They usually plan on what they will do for the first couple of years after retirement, like travel or golf.

Stage Two: Initial Retirement

This is the first two to three years of retirement. While you are working, you cannot wait for the day you can retire. Then, after a few years, the things that you thought you would never get tired of become tiring. It is like being on a strict diet for six months and then eating a large cheese and pepperoni pizza. The first piece tastes the best. If you are anything like me, the first *six* pieces taste good. However, if you had to eat pizza every day you would get sick of it.

If you want to know how to live longer, and have better balance in your life, do not look at retirement as the time that you will stop being productive. The minute you do that is the minute that you start to die. When you do not have a larger purpose in life, you will usually succumb to the commonality of talking about all the negativity in the world, all of which you can do nothing to change.

I love meeting with clients in their seventies that still work. They work not because they have to, but because they love what they are doing. One of your goals could be to become financially set so that you can get a job or start a business in something that you absolutely love. The key is to set it up so you can enjoy all the other goals in life. If one of your goals is to travel four weeks a year, you should get a job or business that will allow you to do it. Most of our retired clients have never considered this as an option. I would suggest that you seriously consider this as one of your goals. If there is any way you can combine some of your goals into a job that you would absolutely love and make money at the same time, what could be better in life?

Now you are ready to start writing out your goals and reviewing the actual goals sheet.

Steps in writing out your goals:

Step 1: Write out all goals

Define all your goals

Step 2: Write down the results you would get from the goal if you achieved it.

What is the personal benefit or result you would get if you attained the goal?

Here is an example:

If one of your goals is to give more time and money to the charity of your choice, what is the personal result that you would get? You might answer something like, "I would feel personally fulfilled that I helped someone less fortunate than I." You might also say, "I feel good because I gave to something bigger than myself." Lastly, you might say, "I was able to invest my time in something I feel very passionate about." **<u>What it is for you… is for you to discover</u>**! This is one of the most important steps. In this first step, people make a mistake when setting their goals. They limit their possibilities because they have never been able to think big.

A second mistake people make when setting goals, is to think too big or too fast and end up getting discouraged. "That all sounds nice if someone gave it to you," I hear a lot. In the real world, the achievement of a goal means you will have to give something in return. If you cannot see the result or the benefit for yourself, most likely you will not be willing to give something in exchange. You will find some things on your list that you wrote down that after you try to find the result or benefit for yourself it just does not feel right. If you have some goals like that, take them off your list.

Step 3: Compare against your list of values

Now take each of your remaining goals and compare them against your list of values. If you attain these goals, will they violate your values or will they coincide with your values? If they violate your values, remove them because your values are your guiding path.

Step 4: Add Dollar Amounts

Now write in the dollar amounts that these goals will cost you. Here is where you get to have fun. Do not guess! If you are guessing at any part of this, it is like shooting at a target blindfolded. DO NOT GUESS!

If your goal is to buy a new car, then go and test-drive the new car. Get the cost for the exact car you want with the cost for each of the options you want. If you want to get electric hurricane shutters for your house, (this is a big one in Florida) then call three contractors and obtain bids. The key with this step is to be as accurate as possible. You will find that when you work with a comprehensive wealth manager (coach) they will expect you to get these costs for your goals. Otherwise, it would be shorting you the experience of getting inspired by physically touching, seeing or understanding your goal.

I will give you an example. In one case, a client wrote down a BMW as one of her goals. She went and test-drove the car. She later called me and said she wanted to take the goal off her list. I asked why. She replied, "I always thought I wanted to own one, but after driving it I actually like my Lexus better. I think I want to put a new Lexus on my list and replace it every three to four years."

Let me give you one more example. One of my newer clients wrote down that they wanted to get involved in a charity. I asked them if they wanted to give money, time or both. They said "just the money". I wanted them to go and check out a few charities they were interested in. I got a call a few weeks later. They said they visited the Children's Cancer Center in Tampa, FL and they were touched by what these children and their families have to go through. They not only wanted to give the money they planned on, but they also wanted me to put in *time* as one of their goals. They told me when they visited, it softened their hearts, and neither of them had a dry eye the rest of the day. I absolutely love to see this kind of passion and purpose unveiled once a person gets personally involved in their goals.

Step 5: Your Due Date

This step involves setting an absolute date for your accomplishment. I have found this is a step where the financial coach (wealth manager) will be of help. Financial sophistication and future value calculations will come into play here. My suggestion is to begin by putting down the dates that you would like to see your goals achieved. Once you meet with a financial coach (wealth manager), be prepared to adjust some of these dates up or down. You will see more about how this works a little later in the book. For now, just write down what you think the dates will be. Some of the dates will be easy if they are based on certain things, such as a minimum retirement age or your children's college education. If you have a ten-year old and one of your goals is to educate your children, your date for achievement will be eight years away. Make sure you are specific!

Many times clients will plan to retire at age sixty-two. I ask what month and they look at me as if I am crazy. I explain that in order to have a *real* plan we need to know the actual month and day that retirement will occur. When it comes to creating a plan, the actual date in time is very important. If you said age sixty-two, there are 365 days that could be your potential target date.

As a financial coach, I require this type of exercise. Leaving this out would be like trying to bake a cake and only adding one egg, when the recipe calls for two.

Step 6: Prioritization

This will be the hardest step by far in your goal-setting strategy. Here is how you have to think of it. If I had to choose between two goals, would I choose one over the other or would I compromise on the amount or the date? Before you get started, I also want to tell you that if you are going to hire a financial coach (wealth manager) you will need to have goals prepared in what I call **Stage 1-Prioritization**. This means that before any financial calculations are done, you are going to give your financial coach (wealth manager) an idea of what you want as a priority and in chronological order. In many cases, our firm has done a plan and found that all the goals are achievable and there is no need to compromise. In other cases, there are not enough financial resources or income to achieve all the goals. Once you are done with **Stage 1-Prioritization** then you need to go to **Stage 2- Compromise**.

Here is an example:

Let us say you have two goals:

1) **To retire at the age of sixty-two**
2) **To fully educate my children for college**

If the financial plan says that you have full potential to achieve your goal to retire at age sixty-two, but the cost for college education reduces your chance for retirement to fifty percent, you have to look at making some changes. One of the changes you can make is to adjust your retirement age. Another is to look at reducing the amount that you want to contribute to the college. If this is the case, you have to plan how the rest of it will be paid. Will college loans, the child or grandchild working, or potential aid do it? You have to compute the financial plan again to see what the potential is. The overall goal with this type of plan is to achieve *one hundred percent* of all your goals. There is no perfect answer! The answer may be in knowing how to make the adjustments. As you start on your path, you will create milestones you have to reach in order to attain these goals. Let us say that you set a target return on your money of eight percent and you only end up earning seven percent by the end of the year. You now have to go back and run the financial planning projections again to see what adjustments will be required. It may mean that you now have to work another year. It may mean that you will have less to provide for the college fund, if you wish to retire before age one hundred. It may mean that you have to reduce the amount of your spending today to achieve both the retirement and/or college goal. It may even mean that you have to look at earning more income to achieve your goal. There are many combinations to reach your goals. The first step is setting the goals, then plan it all out. This is where the financial roadmap comes into place.

Summary:

➤ **Goals need to be inspiring, yet realistic**

Action Steps:

➤ **There are steps in setting your goals -**

1) Identify all your goals.

2) Put dollar amounts and deadline dates on your goals.

3) Check your goals against your values.

4) Prioritize your goals as to importance, then by deadline dates.

The difference between where you are now

and where you want to be

is a plan and the actions to get you there!

CHAPTER NINE

YOUR FINANCIAL ROADMAP

At this point, you should have a very descriptive and compelling list of goals, as well as, all your values identified. Now it is time for you to create a *financial roadmap* so you can clearly see your destination and the path you need to take to get there. At this point, you should look at your financial roadmap like planning a vacation.

When you set out to take a trip, you first decide on the destination. This is the same as setting your values. You start by thinking about past memories or experiences or yearning for new ones. Then you go back to the mental filing cabinet for any files that you have good memories. Then, you decide on the timing, that is, when will you travel? Now you have to decide *how* you are going to get there. Do you want to fly because you want to get there quickly? On the other hand, maybe, you have a fear of flying so you want to drive. Maybe you want total relaxation so you choose a cruise or a train. You can see how much your personal financial plan relates to taking a vacation. Let us look at how you might plan each trip and then you can see your choices when it comes to your personal financial roadmap.

If you decide you want to fly, you have two choices. You can go online and try to research the best rates or you can go to the travel agent. Personally, I would choose the travel agent. I have found that when I am trying to take a nice vacation, the travel agent cannot only find me the best deals but I can give the agent all my travel preferences.

I really do not see how going online and trying to figure it all out on my own would work better. This is what happens when people think they are saving a few bucks by trying to buy investments, insurance, legal services, tax advice, and real estate on their own. I really do not see the savings.

Your other option is to hire a wealth manager (like the travel agent) who will be proactive for you. (In financial terms, this means that you will find a financial coach - wealth manager - and pay for a base plan or hourly). You will have a financial plan (otherwise known as a financial roadmap) created and you will update it each year by being proactive and meeting with your financial coach (wealth manager) once a year. Throughout the year, it is your responsibility to carry out all the annual tasks needed.

Remember, it is not all about just getting there, but how you get there, too. You can go online and find financial products on your own to save a few bucks. (You can buy maps and try to figure it out yourself.) The problem is all the potential pitfalls, such as knowing what kind of products you need, how much or how little you should have, you can really run into some problems. This is why I suggest a financial coach (wealth manager) to help you get to your destination. I hope you can see how, if you find the right financial coach (wealth manager), the trip to your destination can be so much more enjoyable.

Let an expert coordinate all the moving parts, whether it is for travel or with your financial future.

There are some steps to take whether you are going to go at it alone or have some help.

Step 1: Determine your current location

Before you start out on your trip, you have to know your starting point. *You first need to prepare your current financial position. This is the only way you or your financial coach (wealth manager) will know if there is a gap between where you are now and where you want to be.(Otherwise known as the "Gap Analysis").*

Following is a list of all the major financial documents you will need to put together:

- ✓ †Will
- ✓ †Trust
- ✓ †Durable Power of Attorney
- ✓ †Health Care Surrogate

- ✓ †Living Will

- ✓ †All Investment and Retirement Plan Statements

- ✓ †Pension Plan and Social Security Information

- ✓ †Life Insurance

- ✓ †Disability Insurance

- ✓ †Long Term Care Insurance

- ✓ †Health Insurance or Medicare Supplement

- ✓ †Annuity Statements and Policies

- ✓ †EE or Government bonds

- ✓ †Bank account, money market and CD statements

- ✓ †Recent tax returns

- ✓ †Current budget

- ✓ †List of liabilities including -

  - ✓ ☐ Interest rates

  - ✓ ☐ Date loan originated

  - ✓ ☐ Original amount borrowed

  - ✓ ☐ Current balance and term of loan

- ✓ †Specifics on any real estate or business ventures

- ✓ †Purchase date, price, and cost basis

- ✓ †Copies of deeds or business arrangements.

From this exercise, you will also get a much better idea of how well you are organized. Do you have a junk drawer in your kitchen?

Most people, at least if they are honest, say yes. If you have children, you probably have multiple junk drawers. If you are like me, every so often I open the junk drawer and see something that I either thought I lost or completely forget I owned, one of those "oh, that's where that ended up." Unfortunately, the financial lives of some people work the same way. Over the years, people accumulate all kinds of financial products and accounts. Think about all the different *stuff* you have. Can you really remember the reason that you bought it? Was it a decision based on an overall strategy or was it haphazard? Over the years, clients have told me the reasons they have bought stuff. "Oh, my neighbor said he really made a lot of money in this one stock so I bought some." "I really liked the insurance salesperson." In many cases, people hold onto investments and insurance even though their lives have changed, but they have not changed their financial plans or the products and services that support that plan. I hope that when you are done with this exercise you will better understand where you stand financially. You should have a much better idea of your starting point.

Step 2: Set your destination

This is the fun part! Take out your goals sheet. Some of you have read this far and have not participated in any of the exercises. If you do not have your goals sheet completed, please complete it now. You will need to complete it because the next step is to map out your goals in chronological order. We will be writing down what we call your "milestones". In the old days, roads were marked every mile with stones so you would know how far you traveled. If you wrote down that you currently have $10,000 in liquid cash, but you would like $20,000, write down your current stage, then your milestone of $20,000. If you wrote down a time or non-money goal, you have to relate that back to a dollar amount. As an example, if you wrote down, "to take off two months of the year," that relates back to a dollar amount. If you are going to travel during those two months, then put the amount of your travel expenses in as the goal. If you need to take off time and travel, then add the two. If this number, as an example, came to $10,000, then write in $10,000. If you currently have investments that are producing $5,000 per year, you now know the gap that you have to make up. These milestones are to be in chronological order. Remember, at this point, you should only have goals that meet your values and they should be prioritized with dates. The purpose of this financial roadmap is to draw out your current location, where you want to go, and what you expect along the way.

Summary:

➤ Unless you know where you are (financially), it will be difficult to set a path to follow in order to reach your destination.

➤ You must have a destination or ultimate financial goal in mind in order for a plan to be devised.

➤ The theory of "saving the money and doing-it-yourself" can actually be the very way to lose money.

Action:

➤ Decide on how you want to reach your goals, first class (wealth manager), or coach (by yourself)?

➤ Create a timeline of your goals and, specifically, how you want to get to these goals (all the details of the goals).

➤ Decide if you want to try to get to your destination by chance or do you want a roadmap (a written financial plan)?

➤ Determine your current location (financially).

➤ Organize all your financial documents!

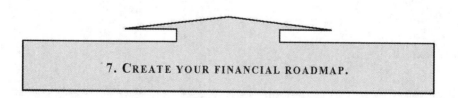

7. CREATE YOUR FINANCIAL ROADMAP.

Obstacles become opportunities, when the

right people join together.

CHAPTER TEN

CREATE YOUR GAP ANALYSIS

After we have laid out where you are starting from (financially), we must now lay out where you want to go. The destination, or financial goals, are extremely important, without them, you would have no direction. Once the starting point and the destination are established, we must find and bridge any gaps that may exist in the plan.

This is where your gap analysis comes into place.

In a recent article by Russ Alan Prince and Hannah Shaw Grove, they stated the following; *The idea of losing their wealth is a top concern of the middle class millionaire. Nearly nine out of ten middle class millionaires (88.6 percent) are very concerned with the potential of no longer affording a lifestyle they have become accustomed to. A substantial number of middle class millionaires are engaging in a financial balancing act. Many of them are often only a few steps away from a significant financial reversal and this places a great deal of pressure on them to maintain their lifestyles and that is where a high quality financial advisor comes in.* ***Taxes.*** *The majority* *of middle class millionaires (84.7 percent) are most interested in mitigating income taxes because of their strong immediate impact. For middle class millionaires (49.2 percent), mitigating estate taxes are very important. At the same time, middle class millionaires (41.7 percent) are very interested in mitigating capital gains taxes. The real problem is that most financial advisors do not understand these concerns.*

If you are going to do all this on your own, you should have a financial planning software program that can make these calculations for you. I would not suggest you try to do this without the software, no matter how proficient you are with spreadsheets or BA55 financial calculators. Your objective is to see how many of your financial goals you will be able to achieve without changing anything. You want to come up with a "base plan". This base plan is what will allow you to analyze any changes that you need to make in order to reach your goals. The base plan shows you how your financial life will look in the future if you make *no* changes.

Here is an example:

John and Teresa came in to see us and their goals were as follows:

1) **To educate their children**

    a. Four years from today with an annual cost of $12,000 for four years for the first child

    b. Six years from today with an annual cost of $12,000 for four years for the second child

2) **To retire and have eighty percent of their combined income to live on, which at the time was $125,000**

    a. To happen in twelve years from today

3) **To assure that if something happened to either one of them that the other person would be able to continue the same lifestyle**

    a. This would mean that ninety percent of the current income of $125,000 would need to be replaced and would have to continue until the children were both out of college and then could drop down to seventy percent of the current income.

4) **To have a vacation home in the mountains**

    a. Current cost of $235,000. They want to have this immediately so they can enjoy time there with their children.

This is their desired destination.

Here is their current starting place:

1) Annual savings of $25,000 to their 401-Ks

2) Current 401-K Balance $323,000

3) Outside investments $425,000 (Stock and funds)

4) Current savings for their children's college $62,150

5) Current life insurance on each of them $250,000

Other Facts:

No other savings besides the 401-K; both have good health; health insurance at work, but no other benefits. We used a three percent inflation rate. We used a rate of return of six percent, which is what their current investment mix has returned on average over the last fifteen years. Current mortgage on home is a variable rate mortgage with a 6.25 percent rate. There are twenty-three years left on the mortgage.

Here is what the gap analysis showed –

Priority	Goal Name	Chance of Success
1	Educate Children	100 percent
2	Retirement	72 percent
3	Financial Security	28 percent
4	Vacation Home	15 percent

(If you are working with a wealth manager or a financial planner, ask them if they base their planning on cash flow planning or on goal achievement).

What this shows is the percentage of potential success if they changed nothing. It takes into account the amount of money they have saved now, the estimated rate of return, inflation, and income taxation.

Educate Children/Retirement

If they educated their children and used part of their money for retirement, it will reduce the chance for success and they will not be able to retire without running out of money. This plan also assumes they live to age ninety. We want to make sure they do not run out of money before they run out of life.

Financial Security

We must look at two scenarios here, if one of them died and/or the other became disabled.

Vacation Home

The vacation home has the lowest probability of success because to buy the house would mean that they would have to drain down their savings and this would reduce their chance of retirement.

As you can see, there is a gap between what they want to achieve and what they will get if they do not make some changes. Where they run into trouble is when they retire and they don't have the money they really need. After all those years of living a nice lifestyle, they will have to make some major adjustments. I have always contended it would be a lot harder to go from a Mercedes-Benz to a Ford Escort than to go from a Ford Escort to a Mercedes-Benz. What usually happens is that they change their thinking entirely. Instead of *enjoying* the retirement years, they go into a protective mode. They become what I call the "living dead". I have seen this so often, it is sad. People stop dreaming and all they do is worry about their money. They sit around the house not wanting to go anywhere and saying, "Oh, it is too expensive to travel. I am on a fixed income and I can't afford that."

Now we are going to bridge the gap by creating the new plan.

Summary:

> ➤ **In order to reach your destination, you must first determine how to get there.**

Action:

> ➤ **Take your financial roadmap of where you are now, and then compute the difference of where you want to be.**
> ➤ **Create your Gap Analysis and determine how to bridge the gap.**
>> o **Minimum amount to be saved**
>> o **Rate of return needed**

- ○ Maximum risk that can be tolerated
- ○ Assets or income that needs protecting by transferring risk to an insurance company
- ○ Determine what other challenges may occur that may prevent the attainment of the goal
- ○ Determine the chances of attainment of the goal (use software to determine)

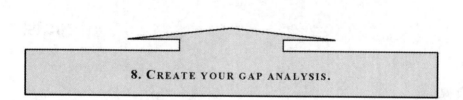

8. CREATE YOUR GAP ANALYSIS.

Obstacles are those frightful things you see when you take your eyes off of your goals.

CHAPTER ELEVEN

CREATE THE INITIAL PLAN

Now that you have your gap analysis, we need to create all the different planning options. Once we have all the options laid out, we can then decide which is best for your specific needs. Let us go back to the same example so you can see how we might do this. (Please remember, I have no idea when you are reading this, so some or all of these ideas may not work. In addition, these ideas have been designed specifically for this client, but would not be recommended to every client, as each recommendation is unique. These examples should never be considered a recommendation to you.)

Scenario 1:

1) Move the children's accounts out of the current accounts since they are Uniform Gift to Minors Act. Move these accounts to 529 programs to eliminate any current income tax on the earnings.

2) Buy the vacation property, but set it up as a rental property. The negative cash flow, even after the rent, will be $1,200 a month or $14,400 a year. Reduce the 401-K by the $14,400

per year. The mortgage payment will create the tax deduction that will be lost by the reduction of the 401-K. The added deductions on the property will save an additional $3,750 a year. (Use this to fund # 3 strategy.)

3) Take the tax savings from the vacation property and buy $1,000,000 of life insurance for each of them, with an annual cost of $3,150. (Covers the financial security goal)

4) Change the investment mix in the 401-K and in the outside investment accounts. Use an asset allocation model with professional (institutional) management. Based on the last fifteen-year performance, the annual net rate of return was 10.17 percent. (Use an alternate lower rate of return (5%) to see if the financial plan can work with the lower rate of return.)

5) Change the mortgage and convert to a fixed rate mortgage with a thirty-year term. By paying down the rate with points, they were able to get 5.75 percent fixed. This saved them $1,525 per year. Take the $1,525 per year and use it to buy disability insurance for both of them. Annual cost- $ 3,100.

6) Set up revocable living trusts for both of them to assure that they eliminate probate and protect children.

Here is the summary:

Saved -

> ➢ $732 in income tax on children's accounts

> ➢ $ 3,750 per year in taxes on vacation home

> ➢ $ 1,525 on mortgage

Total Saved = $6,007

Total Reallocated -

> ➢ New Life Insurance $3,150

> ➢ New Disability Insurance $ 3,100

Total Reallocated = $6,250

Let us look at the new _"WHAT IF"_ plan.

After running the new numbers through the financial planning software, here is what the Gap Analysis showed:

Priority	Goal Name	Chance of Success
1	Educate Children	100 percent
2	Retirement	92 percent
3	Financial Security	100 percent
4	Vacation Home	100 percent

The retirement goal was the only goal that was not 100 percent funded. More changes still needed to be made.

What if Scenario 2:

We reviewed their budget. They agreed that if they wanted to retire at the age of sixty-two then they would have to save more. They came up with a potential budget savings of five hundred dollars per month. We agreed that they would set this up to go into a systematic investment plan to a group of mutual funds.

Now their plan looked like this:

Priority	Goal Name	Chance of Success
1	Educate Children	100 percent
2	Retirement	100 percent
3	Financial Security	100 percent
4	Vacation Home	100 percent

Now they have the chance to live to their highest potential!

Summary:

> ➤ **Once your gap analysis is established, you must then lay out all of your options.**
> ➤ **Remember, there is no right or wrong, only what works best for YOU.**

Action:

> ➤ **Create a list of all your possible options in your plan.**

➢ Test these options against your values and your risk tolerances.

➢ Make final decisions on what opportunities you are going to implement.

9. CREATE YOUR INITIAL PLAN.

The best way to

predict your future,

Is to create it!

CHAPTER TWELVE

CREATE YOUR ACTION LIST

Now that you have determined the plan and the steps you need to take along the path, your next step is to make a list of all the actions or tasks. Then decide who is going to be responsible for each of the tasks.

Following the same example, here is what was on their action list:

1) **Move children's accounts to 529s.**

   a. Research each state's 529 programs

   b. Research the different options within each state

   c. Order account paperwork

   d. Decide on ownership and beneficiary

   e. Transfer existing accounts

   f. Set up measurement and management review for no less than quarterly

2) **Buy vacation property**

   a. Locate realtor in area

   b. Give specification on needs

c. Research all mortgages with emphasis on rates for rental properties

d. Find attorney that can review the contracts, closing statements

e. Compare title insurance companies

f. Find property insurance company

    i. Check ratings and claim paying history

    ii. Compare rates

g. Decide on the proper amount of insurance

h. Decide in what title the property will be bought

    i. Will the husband's trust own it?

    ii. Will the wife's trust own it?

    iii. Should there be a separate LLC set up to protect from lawsuit?

i. Find a property management company

j. Have property management agreement reviewed

k. Set up a separate checking account to handle rental

l. Change 401-K to account for new mortgage payment

    i. Set up special routing account for negative balance for mortgage each month

    ii. Set up review, annually at minimum

          iii. Property management company

          iv. Cash flow statement

3) Buy life insurance

    a. Research insurance companies rates

    b. Research insurance companies ratings

    c. Submit preliminary medical application to get offer

    d. Decide who will be the owner

        i. Should a trust be the owner so the beneficiary is not taxed?

        ii. Should the beneficiary be the spouse or a trust since there are children?

    e. Submit final applications and decide how premiums should be paid and from what accounts

    f. Set up annual review to compare rates against other companies

4) Change investment options in 401-K

    a. Research the investments in the 401-K and sort by each category

    b. In each category, compare available options and choose the optimal investment selections

    c. Contact 401-K and make changes

    d. Set up measurement at least quarterly

      i. Compare the fund performance, turnover, expenses, and category comparison

      ii. Create system that will alert to changes in tolerances in asset allocation model

e. Create model that fits the expected return of 10.17 percent

f. Research all available investment options

      i. Stocks

      ii. Bonds

      iii. Mutual funds

      iv. Closed end funds

      v. Institutional managers

      vi. Exchange traded funds

g. Make changes in current investment mix to conform to the new target model

h. Set up models and allocations so the investments will be tax efficient

i. Set up measurement and management systems

      i. Quarterly review of target model

5) Change the mortgage

a. Research all available mortgages

b. Ask for regulation Z

c. Ask for estimated closing statement

        i. Review closing statement and know which fees can be negotiated

    d. Contact title company to see about credit

    e. Make sure to research tax credit for refinancing mortgage

6) Obtain disability insurance

    a. Research disability companies

    b. Decide if you will put all insurance with one company or split it between two- in case of a denied claim

    c. Compare rate

    d. Compare definitions of disability

    e. Compare riders and options

    f. Compare companies' ratings

    g. Compare companies claim paying percentage

    h. Submit medical application

    i. Put policy in place

    j. Set up system of yearly review

        i. Compare with new rates

        ii. Review companies claim paying ratio

        iii. Review companies rating

7) Set up revocable living trusts

    a. Decide on how you will leave the money upon the first death

b. Decide on how you will leave money to the children

    i. Lump sum

    ii. Annual income

c. Decide on who the trustees will be

d. Decide on which state has the best rules to domicile the trust in

e. Find attorney to draft trust

f. Review draft of trust

g. Get final trust drafted

h. Decide on which assets will go into which trust

i. Make sure that trusts are balanced to assure full use of tax credits

j. Change the titles on the assets to the trusts name

k. Set up system of management

    i. Yearly review of trust distribution provision

    ii. Yearly review of the beneficiaries

    iii. Yearly review with attorney about any trust law changes

8) Set up systematic investment program

a. Find mutual funds that would allow a small monthly investment but would still have good fundamentals and performance

b. Set up funds and decide on the best ownership

c. Create automatic withdraw from checking accounts

d. Create system to rebalance funds every quarter to match the overall asset allocation plan

e. Create system to review the fundamentals of each mutual fund annually and compare

    i. Performance to other managers within same category

    ii. Total risk as compared to other managers in same category

For each one of these tasks you have to decide whether you are going to do it yourself or if you are going to have the financial coach (wealth manager) take care of it for you. When making the decision to do these tasks yourself or have a financial coach (wealth manager) do it for you, keep the following in mind.

To be a wealth manager, you must possess either expertise in or general knowledge in the following:

➢ Debt and Liability Management

➢ Federal Estate Tax Planning

➢ Personal Income Tax Planning

➢ Real Estate Investing and Management

- ➢ Business Income Tax Planning

- ➢ Personal and Business Asset Protection

- ➢ Elder Law (nursing home protections)

- ➢ Investment Management

  - Stock Picking

  - International Investing

  - Tax Strategies

  - Asset Allocation

  - Risk Assessment

  - Performance Measurement

  - Investment Monitoring

- ➢ Retirement Planning

- ➢ College Planning

- ➢ Insurance (each insurance type requires a separate expert).

  - Life Insurance

  - Disability Insurance

  - Health Insurance

  - Auto and Homeowners

  - Business and Liability

- ➢ Distribution Planning

  - IRA's

  - 401K's

Once you have your initial plan set up, then you are going to get into an on going system of measurement and management.

Summary:

➢ **In order to implement the plan you have created you must follow through on the necessary tasks.**

Action: (If you are going to do it yourself)

➢ **Make list of all actions needed to implement your plan.**

➢ **Make list of all companies, people, and products needed to implement your plan.**

➢ **Set timeline for contacting all needed sources.**

Action: (If you are going to hire a wealth manager)

➢ **The wealth manager will complete these tasks for you if this is a part of your agreement.**

10. CREATE YOUR LIST OF ACTIONS.

WHEN A TEAM OF DEDICATED INDIVIDUALS MAKE A COMMITMENT TO ACT AS ONE, THE SKY IS THE LIMIT!

CHAPTER THIRTEEN

Measurement and Management

Have you ever heard the phrase "If it can't be measured, it can't be managed?" One of the most important functions a financial coach (wealth manager) can do for you is to help you stay on track. One of the ways to stay on track is to have a regular system of management. Please do not misunderstand; I am not saying that you should be on your computer checking your stock prices every day. It means that you need a system for *reviewing and measuring* all the different parts of your wealth. *You* should be the one that knows what you want as a result (your goals).

Again, you are the CEO not the CFO. The investment part of your plan should be reviewed no more than annually, if you have structured it correctly. Statistics have shown that rebalancing and changing the investments more frequently than annually only diminishes your returns and increases your risk. *Remember-work smart, not hard.* I would suggest a review of the asset allocation model on an annual basis. Review your tax strategy at the beginning of the year and then again in November/December. The insurance and risk management plan needs to be reviewed once per year, as well as, your cash flow and overall financial roadmap.

Your system of measurement and management should also be as automated as possible. If you are doing this yourself, remember you have a life to live and that does not include spending half your free time organizing and trying to measure and manage your money. One of the keys in an effective measurement and management system is called "Data Aggregation".

Life seems to have gotten more complicated in the last few years. What would you say…has it?

Have you received a credit card offer in your mailbox in the last month? Have you gotten an offer for a home equity loan in the last month? Think about all the paper we now receive. Twenty years ago, we dealt with one or two financial institutions. Typically, we only had one bank and/or one place where all of our investments were held. Now with the Internet, most people have more than five financial institutions. While this system may be better because you can get a slightly better deal on trade costs or interest rates, it becomes almost impossible to manage. When new clients come in, they usually have statements from multiple insurance companies, mutual funds, investment companies, and banks. If I have a hard time looking at all these different moving parts and making good sound management decisions, I can understand how difficult it must be for someone doing it part time. Data Aggregation refers to companies that will go out to all the different financial sources, gather the information, and report it in one simple statement. Few companies offer this service now and you will see the list expanding. We found that for us to manage better we had to create or adopt a system that would data aggregate, for our clients simplicity and for our ability to manage. I would suggest that if you hire a wealth manager; make sure that the individual has a system to consolidate all your information from all the financial institutions.

Include the following:

- ✓ Life Insurance
- ✓ Annuities
- ✓ Investment accounts
- ✓ Retirement accounts
- ✓ 401-Ks and company retirement accounts
- ✓ Company benefits
- ✓ Real Estate
- ✓ Trust accounts
- ✓ Bank and Money Market accounts

Measurement and Management of your Goals

Now that we have spoken about how to measure and manage your financial aspects, let us talk about the most important part of your financial success, the measurement, and tracking of your goals. In the chapter on goal setting, you created your initial goal list. From here on, you and/or your financial coach (wealth manager) will be tracking your goal progression and accomplishments. The most important part of goal tracking is that you and/or your financial coach (wealth manager) are able to track your progression and make adjustments along the way.

One more secret: Once you accomplish a goal, always keep your accomplished goal on your list. This will give you the greatest feeling by looking at all of your accomplishments. It will also boost your confidence level and inspiration to accomplish new goals.

Here is an example of a goals tracking sheet:

Goal Name	Amount	Date Due	Milestone 1 Date and expected result	Milestone 2 Date and expected result	Milestone 3 Date and expected result	Milestone 4 Date and expected result
Pay off debts	$35,000	End of Year				

One of the greatest systems of measurement and management is Weight Watchers. I have had the privilege of seeing how their system is set up. They encourage progression, not perfection, which takes away the stress and gives their customers a great feeling.

They also have you keep a chart of progression, which also keeps your confidence high and is a visual of your achievement. I would highly recommend checking out their system of measurement and management. (www.weightwatchers.com)

Summary:

➢ **If you cannot measure it, you cannot manage it.**

Action:

➢ **Automate as much of your financial life as possible!**

➢ **Automate as much of the measurement and management as possible.**

➢ **Set measurement goals that are within your control.**

➢ **Be ready to adjust your financial plan if you do not achieve certain returns.**

➢ **Do not make certain uncontrollable goals such as rates of return or savings goals (savings goals can be affected by unforeseen emergencies).**

➢ **Strive for progression not perfection.**

➢ **Keep a goals achieved sheet.**

---

11. CREATE A SYSTEM OF MEASUREMENT AND MANAGEMENT.

THE RIGHT TEAM,

WITH A SHARED PURPOSE,

AND A POSITIVE MENTAL

ATTITUDE

CONSTITUTES AN UNSTOPPABLE

FORCE.

CHAPTER FOURTEEN

WHAT ARE YOUR OPTIONS WHEN CHOOSING AN ADVISOR/ COACH

The financial field is unlike the other professional fields in that there is a crossover of Federal, State, and private agencies with regard to regulation. This causes incredible confusion on the part of the consumer. Let me give you an example.

I saw this ad in a recent newspaper advertisement.
9%
GUARANTEED RETURN
Call Now
John Doe Financial Services
All Returns and Principal Guaranteed
John Doe Financial Advisor

What do you know from this ad? Can you tell me what kind of advisor he is? Does the FDIC guarantee this? Is this a stockbroker, a financial planner, or a wealth manager? **Actually, he is none of the above!** This is an ad run by a *local mortgage broker*. As you can see, it is very confusing as to with whom you are dealing. The product he is offering is secured mortgages. Whom is it guaranteed by, he is using the properties as collateral? Is that really a guarantee like the FDIC? No. Nevertheless, how is the consumer to know this? I guess the government thinks that everyone is up on all these issues.

Here is a business card that a client gave me from someone who made a sales pitch to them. Tell me what you think this person does.

John Doe
Financial Planner
USA Financial Services
Member NASD-SIPC

This person is purposing that he is a financial planner. (The Securities and Exchange Commission says that a person cannot hold himself or herself out to be a financial planner unless registered as a financial advisor with the S.E.C.) This person is a registered representative, not a registered investment advisor. What this means is that he is not allowed to charge an hourly fee for advice. He is not allowed to charge a financial plan fee. He is not allowed to charge an asset-based fee. However, he is allowed to sell mutual funds, stocks, life insurance, and annuities. Before I go any further, I am going to give you the best advice of your life. I am going to let you in on a secret of whom you should really deal with. Are you ready- IT ALL DEPENDS ON WHAT YOU WANT!

Repeatedly, I pick up financial publications and from one publication to the next, they will negatively blast one discipline in the financial industry or another. *Either the people who earn commissions are all thieves or the people who charge hourly rates are all charging too much,* all to get you to lean towards whoever is throwing out the negative information so you will choose them for your business. It is like a negatively run political ad campaign. I get sick to my stomach when November comes around and the politicians start in with the he said/she said negative publicity blast. This happens the same way in the financial services industry. I think that it really does a disservice to the entire industry. What this does is create a distrust for the entire financial services industry. In my experience, I have met many financial planners, advisors, brokers, and even politicians that I would trust with my financial future. Many people could use the help of a financial professional, but they try to do it themselves because of a lack of knowledge of with whom to deal.

I am going to help you understand who is available, how they charge, the negatives and the positives. I hope that this will help you understand how to choose the right advisor/coach. Please understand, while you are reading this I will do the best I can to help you understand the positives and the negatives. I may have left some points out, not on purpose.

I am not recommending one over the other. This is simply to help you understand. However, I will put some caution flags in so you know where you should express caution. At the end of this chapter, you will be provided with a checklist of questions to ask of the advisor/coach you will be working with. The information below is so you will better understand the checklist found later. The checklist is more important to make your decision than to choose based on the information below.

Let us start with the types of firms or companies with which you can work:

1. **Broker Dealer (Wire Houses)**
2. **Independent Broker Dealers**
3. **Discount Brokers**
4. **Registered Investment Advisor Firms (custodial)**
5. **Registered Investment Advisors (non-custodial)**

Broker Dealer (Wire Houses)

These are usually your large companies such as Bank of America, Sun Trust, Merrill Lynch, etc. You get the idea. They are set up with many support services such as administrative staff, research departments and usually have good technology for their accounts. These companies are usually regulated by the NASD (a self-regulatory arm sanctioned by the Securities and Exchange Commission to regulate certain broker dealers), the New York Stock Exchange, or other exchanges. They are not directly regulated by the S.E.C.

Positives:

1) You have a large company

2) You usually have multiple services to choose from

3) You have systems and procedures in place that can reduce any wrong doing

4) You could have banking combined with investment services

5) You usually have the ability to move from one advisor/ coach to another if you are unhappy

Negatives:

1) You have a large company (Same as under a positive because there is good and bad with having a large company) I put this as a negative because I personally like dealing with smaller companies that won't put me into "ignore mode" after I have gone through twenty selections on their voice mail system. This is a personal preference.

2) Many of these companies are sales organizations first, and wealth management, or investment services, second. Some have created teams that are not a part of the sales organizations.

3) Many of these companies have proprietary investments that they sell that may carry higher commissions, loads, or fees.

4) Many of these companies hire people to get their basic license only. Being certified is usually not a mandatory requirement.

5) Fees are sometimes hidden. Many mutual funds, annuities, or other products are not required by law to tell you up front about their fees. Some companies require you sign disclosures, but it is not the law to do so. This is not bad that they charge fees, but the average consumer does not know where to find the fees and make a good comparison.

6) They are not required by law to tell you about any conflicts of interest. If they are receiving special deals to sell a product or getting something called soft dollars they don't have to disclose it. Soft dollars are monetary incentives they may get back from the

vendors they are dealing with. They legally do not have to tell you.

7) Your accounts are usually considered to be owned by the company. If your advisor decides to change companies or go independent, it usually causes either a legal battle or hassles for you. This can be a real problem because you usually have the relationship with the advisor and not the company.

8) Usually their fees are higher than average to pay for all the overhead. If you are using all the extra services, it may be worth it to you.

Independent Broker Dealers

These are companies such as Pershing, LPL or, depending on when you are reading this; it could be thousands of the other companies that are considered Broker Dealers. These companies cater to registered representatives that are independent, which will be explained shortly. These companies act as custodian by holding your investments and sending you statements. They also act as the place that will make the trades for your investments. They normally do not have their own products, but rather act as a broker to offer the RR (Registered Representative) a place to get multiple products. They will usually have a menu of products such as stocks, bonds, mutual funds, variable annuities, life insurance, etc. These companies are usually regulated by the NASD (a self-regulatory arm sanctioned by the Securities and Exchange Commission to regulate certain broker dealers) or by the New York Stock Exchange or other exchanges. They are not directly regulated by the S.E.C.

Positives:

1. Usually independent and do not have the goal of selling a certain product

2. Usually have a good technology system to give you information on taxes and consolidated statements

3. Usually have a good menu of products for the RR, from which to choose

4. You are going to be dealing with a RR that may be independent, which may allow a more independent view of what you should own

Negatives:

1. Because the broker is generally located in one city and the RR is located in another, the oversight is not what it usually is in a large brokerage house. This should not necessarily worry you, but it is a negative on my list.

2. Fees are usually hidden. Many mutual funds, annuities, or other products are not required by law to tell you up front about their fees.

3. They are not required by law to tell you about any conflicts of interest. If they are receiving special deals to sell a product or getting kickbacks (otherwise known as soft-dollars), they legally do not have to tell you.

4. Many of the RRs come from a large brokerage house and are still in sales mode as opposed to a planning mode.

5. In some cases, the broker dealers work on a "subscription only" basis. This means that if you buy five different mutual funds from five different companies you are going to be getting five different statements. Again, this will make it very hard for you to measure and manage your situation.

Discount Brokers

Discount brokers are companies like E-Trade, TD Waterhouse Retail, and Schwab Retail. By the time you read this book some of these companies may have already been consolidated and merged. The purpose of these companies is to deal with the do-it-yourself investors. These companies are usually regulated by the NASD (a self-regulatory arm sanctioned by the Securities and Exchange Commission to regulate certain broker dealers) or by the New York Stock Exchange or other exchanges. They are not directly regulated by the S.E.C.

Positives:

1) Most of the time they will give you the lowest trade costs

2) They usually have good technology since as a do-it-yourself investor, you need Internet access

3) Usually you do not have sales people that will attempt to sell you products that may not fit your needs

Negatives:

1) You have to figure it all out yourself. If you buy something and you lose money, you are the responsible one.

2) They usually have very poor tax tools. This means you have to understand all the tax rules.

3) Numerous studies have been done, in which investors that trade their own accounts usually do worse, than with a broker or advisor. Statistically, it has been shown that the more you tinker with and try to outwit the market, the worse you will do.

4) You have to be very careful with your technology. A recent Business Week article (November 2005) talked about how people have hacked into peoples' home computers and transferred money out of their online brokerage accounts. This is usually not possible with the first two options as they generally do not offer online money transfers or you have a personal advisor that may notify you of odd transactions.

*In a recent article in the November 14 issue of Business Week by Amy Borrus, she showed what the risks are with some online brokerage accounts. **Invasion of the stock hackers.** Arriving home from a five week trip to Belgium and India on Aug 14th 2005, a jet lagged Korukonda L. Murty picked up his mail and got the shock of his life. Two monthly statements from online brokerage E*Trade Financial Corp showed that securities worth $174,000, the bulk of his and his wife's savings, had vanished. During July 13-26, stocks and mutual funds were sold and the proceeds wired out of his account in six transactions of nearly $20,000 a piece. Murty, a 64 year old nuclear engineering professor at North Carolina State Univ, could only imagine that this was a mistake. He had not sold any stock in months. His home computer lacked antivirus software and had been infected with code that enabled hackers to grab his user name and password. Then they had the brokerage wire the proceeds to a phony account in his name at Wells Fargo Bank.*

Registered Investment Advisors (custodial)

(Please read the end of this section to understand the difference between a custodial and a non-custodial RIA.)

These companies are directly regulated by the S.E.C. They receive their audits directly by S.E.C. auditors. An RIA firm must also file what is called an ADV Part II and update it annually. This form outlines how they charge their fees, what conflicts of interest they might be involved in, how exactly they manage investments, how often they review your accounts, and how often they meet with you. The form ADV typically outlines exactly what you can expect in services and in costs. It is what I would refer to as, the transparency test. It would be like going to your doctor and getting a form that would tell you his education, the education of his staff, how he determines recommending tests, and if he owns or receives profit from any of the testing facilities that he sends you. Does he get a free game of golf by any pharmaceutical reps? Has he ever been sued and what was the outcome or does he have any complaints against him?

The differences between an RR and a RIA

The difference between dealing with a RR and an RIA is that the RIA must provide this form to you before you agree to do business with them. When dealing with a RR you would have to dig out all this information on your own. An RIA firm can employ RRs. Some RIA firms' employees or advisors might also have relationships with independent broker dealers. This might allow them to use not only pay for advice services like asset management, financial plans or hourly consulting, but if they see the use for life insurance, long term care insurance, mutual funds or annuities, they might be able to use them. It is a misconception that commissions are an awful thing. In some cases, it is less expensive to deal with a commission product than with a no load product that the advisor will be charging you an asset based fee. It is not a matter of whether it is commissions vs. fees. What is important, however, is that the person you are dealing with is looking at all angles and using what is best for you, instead of what is best for him or her.

A custody RIA means that they will be holding your money and investments under their control.

Positives:

1) Transparency. You can see all the fees, and/or conflicts of interest. You can see exactly how they work and what to expect.

2) They usually are not in the business of selling a product

3) They do not have proprietary products like mutual funds or variable annuities with higher fees.

4) They are usually independent, which means that they are working for you instead of for a big company.

5) They are your coach/advisor and do not have to split their commitments between meeting sales goals and doing the best thing for you.

6) They typically have smaller firms and therefore have fewer turnovers. You usually create long lasting relationships with the staff and, since they understand you and your situation, you have a better chance of getting more personal help.

Negatives:

1) Fees are transparent. Why is this negative? I have actually had people tell me they did not like seeing their fees. When they owned mutual funds, they thought they did not have any fees. I hope you understand that all mutual funds have fees. Sometimes it does not hurt as bad when you do not see them, but they are still there. In any case, you might be happier not seeing the fees.

2) The RIA firm may not be stable and since they are holding your money, you need to be very careful of solvency. (For Custodial Firms ONLY)

3) They usually do not have the technology that the large brokerage companies have.

4) They usually have smaller staff so you have to understand what they will provide and what they will not.

Registered Investment Advisors (Non-Custodial)

Everything is the same as the previous definition except they do not hold your money. They will usually let a large company such as Fidelity, Schwab, Ameritrade, or TD Waterhouse hold onto your money. This way you are getting the benefits of a large company with the personal service and attention of an individual or team that personally knows you. That should give you a good foundation to understanding the types of companies that you can deal with.

Now let us look at the types of advisors with whom you can work:

1) Registered Representative (RR)
2) Investment Advisory Representative (IAR)
3) Agent
4) RR/IAR/Agent

The Registered Representative (RR)

An RR must first pass a license exam to be able to sell investment products. It is very, very important to understand that the law states that an RR MAY NOT RENDER INVESTMENT ADVICE OR FINANCIAL PLANNING.

This may be contrary to everything you have heard. The law is extremely murky on this issue and it not only confuses the consumer, but also, many financial institutions.

An RR is allowed to tell you about and explain investment products. They are not supposed to give you investment advice. As you will see later, the checklist will help you determine with whom to deal. Do not get hung up on whether the person can render advice. I have personally met some incredible RRs that help their clients get to their goals and they only work on commission. I have also met some RIAs that care nothing about their clients. It is important to understand that an RR works on commissions. Again, this is not a bad thing if the person has your best interests in mind. The RR is also not required to give you all the ways he or she makes money, nor are they required to tell you about any problems they have had in the past or any conflicts of interest.

The Investment Advisory Representative

The IAR works for an RIA (Registered Investment Advisory Firm). In certain states like Florida, they do have to pass a test. In other states, they must only file a form with either the Federal Government or the State. They also must give you the form ADV Part II by either physically giving it to you or giving it to you by electronic form (via email or on a CD.)

Agent

This is usually an insurance agent. They obviously work only on commission by selling a product. They usually have to pass a test and keep up to date with continuing education. I know many of these people have really taken the brunt of the jokes, but let me tell you, they are important. I do not hear any of those jokes when a spouse dies. I do not hear any of those jokes when someone becomes disabled or has a large medical insurance claim. I did not hear any of those jokes after the hurricanes hit Florida. Agents serve a very important part of our financial community. It goes back to the same universal rule: **Are they doing things in your best interest?** Either you are an expert on insurance or you have a quarterback, otherwise known as your wealth manager or financial coach, to oversee what the agents are doing. I think a majority of the jokes should be reserved for those agents that sell products to people that should not have them or cannot afford them.

RR/IAR/Agent

This person holds licenses for being an RR, IAR, and insurance agent. These people are usually well versed and, most of the time, work in the wealth management field. They are usually a wealth manager that has the knowledge to oversee a team of people doing all these tasks.

It needs to be mentioned again, the quality of your relationship and your potential success does not depend on the type of company you deal with; it depends on the type of advisor/coach you are working with. You could have a very educated advisor that is technically gifted, yet will still fail. Why? The advisor is like Mary's Hamburger Business, as opposed to McDonalds. They do not have a system that will regiment, measure, and manage your progression towards your goals. The type of company and the type of coach/advisor is only one of the areas to understand, but not the only factor to consider in your decision.

One of the areas of confusion is how you pay and what you pay to an Investment Advisor. Earlier, you learned that the RR (Registered Representative) earns a commission. The commission is not negotiable because the companies set it. It is illegal for the RR to give you back or agree to reduce the commission in any way. I have noticed a great misunderstanding when it comes to hiring a Registered Representative, who is also a Registered Investment Advisor.

There are different types of investment advisors and each of them offers a different level of service:
   1) Investment Management Only
   2) Financial Planning Only
   3) Comprehensive Wealth Managers

Investment Manager

An **Investment Manager** is a Registered Investment Advisor, but only performs a certain duty and that is to invest your money. It is not their job to understand your estate plan, your retirement plan, your insurance, or any of the other moving parts of your total financial picture. In many cases, their fees will run from .50 percent to 3 percent depending on what type of investment management they are providing. If you have a manager that is investing in index funds (a way to invest without having to try to depend on picking the right markets, managers, or investments) and is operating your asset allocation model, you should expect to pay between .80 percent and 1.50 percent. If they are using mutual funds, which requires more research into the fund managers and tracking their performance, you should expect to pay between .50 percent and 1.5 percent, depending on how much you have the investment advisor manage. The lower the amount of investment, the higher percentage you pay. If the investment manager is working with individual equities, you should expect to pay a higher rate, as they are now required to do all the research on the investments themselves. Between 1 percent and 2.5 percent depending on how much you have under management. If they are dealing with any advanced techniques, such as selling covered calls, then expect to pay more.

The problem has been that many people will compare investment managers' fees but not ever consider how the manager is managing the money. Keep in mind that investment management on its own is quite different from wealth management. You can usually expect to pay a fee either annually or on a quarterly basis. The fees I just mentioned are on an annual basis so if you are billed quarterly then divide the fee by four.

Financial Planners

Financial Planners will charge you differently, depending on how they are set up. Some are set up only to create the financial plan. In most cases, you can expect to pay a flat fee, an hourly fee, or a fee based on the complexity of the plan. In these cases, you have to know whether the financial planner is only going to write the plan for you or if they will write the plan and then help you implement it. You should know this before you agree to the plan. If they help you implement the plan, will there be additional fees or will they work off commissions from financial products? The estimated cost for a financial plan can run between five hundred dollars and twenty-five thousand dollars, depending on the complexity of the plan. Beware of anyone offering you a free financial plan. When people tell me they have had financial plans done, my first question is, "Was it for free?" If it was, there is a very good chance that it was done by someone who was only interested in selling a product. In most cases, the financial plan is skewed toward whatever the financial product is. When you are looking for a financial planner, you also have to decide whether you want just the plan done or if you want to work with someone over the long term. If you want just the plan done that means that you have to work as the general contractor and put all the sub contractors together to build the plan.

The plan is only the blueprint; someone still has to put up the building.

Comprehensive Wealth Manager

A wealth manager is usually a financial planner that is also registered as an investment advisor. This means that they tend to be the ones that will draw the financial plan. Again, be careful of the FREE financial plan. I do not know of any highly qualified wealth managers that will draw a financial plan for you with only the hopes that you might bring your entire management to them. You should expect to pay for a financial plan. The wealth manager is equipped to help you not only implement the action tasks in the plan, but also act as your advisor/coach over your lifetime. You can use the estimated costs for a financial plan that I listed under Financial Planner for the same estimated fees for set-up of the financial plan. Once the financial plan is completed, then some wealth managers may charge you an additional implementation fee or will include the implementation fee when you agree to hire them as your full time advisor/coach. A wealth manager will charge you under a number of different methods. Some will choose to charge you on an hourly basis. I would not suggest this. The reason is that everything is *reactive* as opposed to *proactive*. What usually happens is you will get to meet with them maybe once a year. You meet with them like the CPA, in other words, you tell them everything you did over the last year. They tell you everything you did wrong and then they tell you what to do over the next year. An example of this is like going on vacation. If you left knowing to go north and you simply stopped at each gas station to ask if you are still going north, it is going to take you a long time to get there and you are going to be misguided along the way.

The second way they can charge you is to charge you an investment-based fee. This usually means that they will manage all your investments along with your overall wealth. At this point, it needs to be clarified again that an investment-only manager is looking solely at your investments. A Comprehensive Wealth Manager is looking over your investments, your insurance, your wills and trusts, your asset protection, and your tax strategies. Most importantly, they are organizing all these moving parts into one efficient and optimal plan. In the past, the only way that wealth managers would charge you was to charge you an investment-based fee. This means that their fees were based on your liquid investment value alone. What many wealth managers have found is that this way of charging you does not really align you with the full value that they are giving you.

As an example, let us say your total net worth is $2,000,000. It consists of $1,000,000 in investments, $500,000 from your home, and $500,000 from one rental property. If the wealth manager charges you, say 1.25 percent, it is only based on the $1,000,000 that you have. Yet they are actually helping you manage $2,000,000. Only about twenty percent of your total discussions will be about the investments that you are compensating them for. Many of your discussions, analysis, and time invested will be on trusts, distribution strategies, retirement planning, asset protection, tax strategies, insurance strategies, etc. In many of the industry publications, advisors talk about the time and effort they put into comprehensive wealth management, yet when they talk to clients, they are comparing the investment returns compared to the fees. In trying to better align the clients understanding of the value the wealth manager brings, many wealth mangers have gone to a "total worth fee". Since the wealth manager is advising, coaching, and helping you with all parts of your wealth, this may be the new wave of the future. As an example, instead of charging 1.25 percent on the investments, you might see a charge of .60 percent, but it is based on your total worth.

I personally think this is a better way that wealth managers can set themselves apart from investment-only managers.   A comprehensive wealth manager helps you increase your overall net worth as opposed to the investment-only manager who is working on just your investments.

Which one is right? I do not know. I think that you have to decide what you want as the result and what you think is important. The decision should be made based on what you learn and believe in after you have gone through the questionnaire that follows.

Summary:

- ➤ **Know what type of company you are dealing with.**
- ➤ **Know the difference between -**
    - o **Broker Dealer (Wire House)**
    - o **Independent Broker Dealer**
    - o **Discount Broker**
    - o **Registered Investment Advisor (custodial)**
    - o **Registered Investment Advisor (non-custodial)**
- ➤ **Know the difference between -**
    - o **A registered representative and an investment advisor representative**
    - o **A commission-only, fee-only, and a fee and commission advisor**
- ➤ **Do you know which type of advisor owes you a fiduciary responsibility and which one does not?**

➢ **Know the difference between -**

  o **A financial planner**

  o **An investment manager**

  o **A comprehensive wealth manager**

12. OPTIONAL – IF YOU ARE GOING TO WORK WITH A COACH- HOW TO FIND ONE.

THE POWER OF A LEADER

TRUE LEADERS ARE NOT THOSE WHO STRIVE TO BE FIRST BUT THOSE WHO ARE FIRST TO STRIVE, AND WHO GIVE THEIR ALL FOR THE SUCCESS OF THE TEAM. TRUE LEADERS ARE FIRST TO SEE THE NEED, ENVISION THE PLAN, AND EMPOWER THE TEAM FOR ACTION. BY THE STRENGTH OF THE LEADER'S COMMITMENT, THE POWER OF THE TEAM IS UNLEASHED.

CHAPTER FIFTEEN

HOW TO CHOOSE THE RIGHT ADVISOR/COACH FOR YOU

This questionnaire is here simply to help you determine what is important to you when choosing a financial coach. There is no right or wrong answer! You should first rate how important each thing is by giving each question a score from one to five. A five is the most important, while a one is the least.

Question	1	2	3	4	5
Does the advisor work for a large company?	○	○	○	○	○
Is the advisor independent?					
How long has advisor been doing this? (Minimum should be five years)					
What other experience does the advisor have? If you are working with someone who owned a business, they may be more educated on business matters.					
How is the advisor regulated? (NASD/ SEC)					
Would you be a client of the advisor/ coach or is your account considered to be owned by the company or firm?					

What happens to you if he/she dies, becomes disabled, retires, or sells his/her business?					
What licenses does the advisor have?					
What certifications does the advisor have?					
Does the advisor belong to any industry organizations or associations?					
Does the advisor charge hourly, asset based, planning fees, or commissions?					
Does the advisor have any disciplinary history?					
Are there any conflicts of interest?					
Will they custody the funds or will it be at a large custodian? Who is the custodian?					
How will you get reports and what type of reports?					
How often will you get reports?					
What are the trade fees of the custodian?					
What is the investment philosophy of the advisor? Asset Allocation, Market Timing, or Security Selection?					
Does the advisor do the investment management or does he/she outsource to professional managers?					
If advisor does his/her own investment management, then how will they find time to work on your goals and financial planning?					

Do they have inside advisors like insurance agents, investment advisors, and tax experts or do they outsource this?					
How often will you get updates on your overall plan and achievement of your goals?					
Will you be working directly with this coach/advisor or do they have a team that will be helping you?					
What technology do they have? Can they aggregate all your investments and insurance into one simple statement?					
How many clients does the advisor have? Usually a single advisor without staff cannot handle more than twenty clients. However, with each staff member, they can handle another twenty-thirty clients. This also depends on what type of advisor they are. If they are a wealth manager, then the rules above apply. The less services they provide, the more clients they can handle.					
Ask for their list of values, their mission, and purpose statement. Evaluate it and see if it matches what you are looking for. If they don't have one, be careful. How can they guide you if they cannot guide themselves?					

Obviously, this is a list that you can add to, but be careful that you only add questions that will evaluate their ability to help you reach your goals. If you gave me the choice of working with different advisors, I would choose the one that had a system and processes, as opposed to having the best product, highest returns, or best education.

What about shopping for a wealth manager that has the lowest fees? The first thing that comes to mind is something Dan Sullivan (from The Strategic Coach) told me, "The most important investment you can make with your money is to buy talent to help you grow."

(You should really read Dan Sullivan's latest book "The Laws of Lifetime Growth", by Dan Sullivan and Catherine Nomura.)

If it was your goal to win a marathon, would you want to hire the least expensive coach or the one that will help you finish and win? Keep in mind that sometimes the lowest fee will mean the lowest service. This often means that you will have to spend more time and have more frustration in your journey. I hope by now, in your life you have realized that the lure of lower fees usually has consequences that you will end up paying for later. Now that you have a basic checklist of how you can find your coach, let us review how you can work better with your advisor/coach.

Summary:

➤ **When choosing a financial coach, you must decide what is important to YOU and YOU alone!**

Action:

➤ Evaluate your potential financial coach/advisor/wealth manager based on who they are, how they work, and how you will work together.

➤ Do not ask for their investment performance because you can take any slice in time and make performance look good or bad.

➤ Find out more about their investment philosophy, as well as, their system and process to investing and managing your money.

➤ Be careful if they profess to have better returns than others. You are hiring this person to get you to your goals, not to get the highest rate of return. With the highest rate of return, you get the highest risk.

➤ Do not evaluate the advisor/coach primarily on fees. In many cases, I have seen some financial coaches that charge upwards of two to three percent, but they are so creative that they save more than that on just the client's tax returns. Then the client gets them for all the rest of their services.

- Look at your relationship like a partnership or marriage – communicate and be open about things you like and dislike.
- Layout your expectations and understand the advisor's expectations.

Notes

COMMUNICATION

Let us build bridges, not walls...

CHAPTER SIXTEEN

HOW TO WORK WITH YOUR ADVISOR/ COACH

Imagine the patient that shows up at the doctor's office to find out why she has been feeling so tired. The doctor walks in the room and asks about her symptoms. The patient says she has no energy and would like to have a prescription written. The doctor says before he gets to that he would like to run some tests to see what is wrong. The patient says, "No forget all that stuff, and just write me a prescription".

As silly as that sounds, this can happen with financial advisors and financial coaches with clients every single day. Many advisors actually will make recommendations without the proper information just to keep the client happy. On the other hand, in some cases, the client asks for advice without providing the proper information. This is not how you get the best value from your financial coach. When you go to see your coach or, if you have a phone conference, be prepared! Find out what your agenda is going to be for your meeting and be prepared.

Depending on how your advisor/coach is set up, also respect their time. If the advisor has a staff of people to help him or her then use the staff. While you might feel most comfortable dealing with the advisor, if they have a staff, do not ininundate the advisor with tasks and questions that their staff can handle. This is the same as calling your doctor's office and demanding that you speak with the doctor about a mistake on your bill. If you want to get the best financial advice, let the financial advisor/coach (wealth manager) invest their time working with your goals, your future, and staying educated. I can tell you, it is very time consuming just to stay up on the changes that are happening all around us. When you are paying a financial advisor/coach (wealth manager), you are not just paying for what they are actually doing for you. You are also getting all their education, experience, and their time they have invested in keeping up to date on everything. The old saying, that you can get more with honey than vinegar holds true with whomever you are dealing.

COMMUNICATE COMMUINCATE COMMUNICATE

Look at your relationship with your advisor/coach as a partnership. You need each other. In any partnership, there should be good communication. If you are expecting something and you are not getting it, it should be your responsibility to go to the advisor/coach and explain that you were expecting something and you do not feel like you received it. At that point, it should be the responsibility of both of you to review the expectations and, if the advisor does not think they can deliver, you have to review how important your expectation is. This should be compared with what else you are getting in comparison to this one expectation.

Referrals

The best compliment that you can give to your advisor/coach is to provide him/her with referrals. I think this really shows your commitment to your partnership. In most advisory firms, about eighty percent of the advisor's time is spent meeting and finding clients. This is less time they can spend on getting you to your goals or getting educated for you. By finding out what the advisor/coach's desired type of client is, you can keep your eyes and ears open for people that might be ideal for the advisor. When we initially meet with clients, we explain that the fees we charge to manage their assets and wealth are only fifty percent of how we are paid. The other fifty percent is through their referrals to us. This has made such a dramatic impact that now eighty percent of all our new clients come from referrals! What this has allowed us to do is to switch the tables. Instead of spending eighty percent of our time looking for new clients, we now spend eighty percent of our time working on current clients' portfolios, financial plans and personally meeting with them.

I see our firm not just as a business, but also as a lifetime missionary. I see the advice and guidance that we give to people, change their lives. I see it creates more quality time with family and I see people's health improve. All this from helping people manage their wealth; make wise money decisions and getting them to their goals. The referrals we get enable us to spread the word and help more people.

Ask your advisor/coach what their mission is, what are they trying to accomplish? They should be *eating their own cooking* and have their own list of values and goals. If their goal is to help large numbers of people, and one of your values is to help people, you can do this by referring people to the advisor/coach. Look at it this way. If a doctor had discovered a way to help you prolong your life, improve your health, and reduce your stress, would you tell everyone about him/her? Find out if your advisor takes accepts new clients and what his/her requirements are for new clients.

Summary:

- ➢ **You are building a relationship.**
- ➢ **Remember, while working with your financial coach, it is imperative to communicate.**

Action:

- ➤ Look at your relationship with your financial coach like a partnership in which both parties must openly communicate.
- ➤ Do not expect unrealistic outcomes from your financial coach.
- ➤ Your financial coach, like you, can only control certain things.
- ➤ Grade the coach on the outcomes they can control.
- ➤ Respect the coach's time and realize they are most valuable to you doing what they do best and that is usually not administrative or paperwork issues.
- ➤ Be willing to work with the coach's staff and allow the coach to focus time on what will give you the best outcome.
- ➤ Realize that you are not only paying for the coach's specific advice, but also for their experience and their ongoing education to keep your plan up to date and provide innovative ideas.
- ➤ If you are satisfied, refer others to your coach, which allows them to spend more time on your plan, rather than looking for new clients.

TEAMWORK

COMING TOGETHER IS A BEGINNING;

KEEPING TOGETHER IS PROGRESS;

WORKING TOGETHER IS SUCCESS!

CHAPTER SEVENTEEN

<u>Wealth Management Teams</u>

What is the new terminology we are hearing about throughout the financial media? You now see it in print ads, TV, and radio. What is a wealth manager? What is a wealth management team? A wealth manager is a person or a team of people that work on all four parts to your financial puzzle. Those four parts are:

- ✓ **Estate and Distribution Planning**
- ✓ **Proactive Tax Planning**
- ✓ **Insurance and Asset Protection**
- ✓ **Investment and Retirement Planning**

In the past, our industry has had an "estate planner". This is a certain type of discipline that is based on the assumption that there is or will be an estate tax levied by our government. The common understanding was that if you had a large estate, you needed an estate planner. The problem was that most people, even those with multiple millions did not consider themselves worthy of an estate planner. It has a lot to do with the definition we put on certain words or titles. I have to admit the first thing that comes to mind when I hear ***ESTATE*** is Robin Leech on the lawn of some movie star's thirty million dollar "Estate".

Each one of us has a different definition for words and that can be a bad thing. Look at how much the government has collected in estate taxes from unwitting people. If they had done some estate planning, they could have paid zero in tax! Since the 2000 election, there has been the unknown future of estate taxes so many people have lost interest in trying to plan for their estate. While the estate tax may or may not stay, it is a fact that most people want their money to pass down to their children and then their grandchildren. In other words, they want their money to stay in the bloodline. This means that while you may not consider estate planning necessary, it is necessary just to preserve your assets and make sure that they will stay in your bloodline. If there is an estate tax and the wealth manager is able to help you reduce or eliminate the tax, it is an added benefit for your children and/or family.

C.W.M. (Comprehensive Wealth Management)
Just what is a wealth manager or wealth management team?
It is the coordination and optimization between all your different moving parts of your financial life.

This term, wealth, means different things to different people. The one thing for sure is everyone has wealth. Your wealth is different from the next woman, but you do have wealth. You may not think you are wealthy, but what you consider as your assets, is your wealth.

The following is a visual of what a wealth manager should be coordinating:

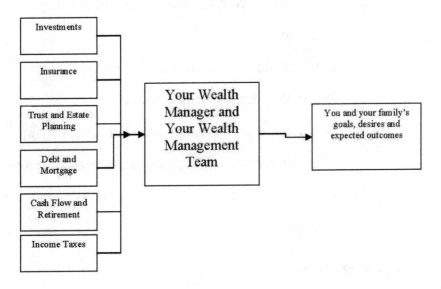

Now that you have a better idea of what wealth management is, let's help you understand wealth management teams.

Here is an example of the job position usually in a wealth management firm.

Financial Architect

Their job is to meet with you and fully understand your goals and values. They convert your current plan into a blueprint for your future.

    a. They should be certified in the discipline that they are practicing.

        i. If you are having an estate plan done, they are usually a certified estate planner.

        ii. If you are having a financial plan done, they are usually certified as a financial planner, a senior advisor, a retirement planning advisor or the like.

Financial Planner

Their job is to help the financial architect create the financial plan. They are usually certified as a financial planner. They generally are like the property managers in that, once the plan is done, their job is to oversee the plan and the attainment of your goals.

Portfolio Manager

They are the ones responsible for keeping track of all your investments and overseeing the performance of the individual investments or the managers. In many cases, you will not usually meet with the portfolio manager. His or her job is to work in the background and to create and oversee the portfolios and work with the financial planner or financial architect.

Client Administrative Assistant

This is usually your personal liaison. They are the ones responsible for taking care of all your administrative or technology needs.

Summary:

➢ **Realize that no one person can be an expert in all the areas of wealth management and, therefore, a good team is necessary.**

➢ **Wealth management means the optimization and coordination of all the moving parts of your financial life-**
  o **Estate and distribution planning**
  o **Proactive income tax planning**
  o **Investment and retirement planning**

o   Insurance and asset protection

Action:

- ➢ Strive to understand what each person does on the team so you are dealing with the right person for the right question or task.
- ➢ Understand that the purpose of the team is to allow you to focus on what you want to do.
- ➢ Be careful of the advisor/coach that does not have a team behind him or her and professes to be able to handle it all for you.

Notes

If you can dream it, you can do it!

Walt Disney

CHAPTER EIGHTEEN

<u>Final Checklist</u>

This book was written with twenty plus years of experience in working with women. I hope that, if you are a do-it-yourselfer, you now understand the systematic process to elevate your life to its' optimal value and to start making wise money decisions.

I hope more than anything, you now understand that you do not have to do it alone! You can attain your goals by working with the right advisor/coach. I cannot emphasize enough that any person that has reached any point of success has done it with the help of coaches and advisors. You now have the ammunition and the information to find and work with the best of the best advisors/coaches!

In closing, I hope that you will now understand that for what you pay to an advisor/coach (wealth manager), you can improve the quality of your life. I hope you will take my advice and find someone that can help you. It is not my intention to try to get you to do business with me, but it is my intention to have you understand the power of working with a trusted advisor and find someone.

Whether it is our firm, or someone else, just find someone that you trust to help you.

My life's mission is to help improve the quality and financial security of all those I meet. I want those of you that I have been able to share this wisdom with to utilize it, enable it to organize and optimize your financial life so that you can enjoy every minute here on earth!

<u>Here is a checklist that I hope you will follow in your quest to improve the quality and financial security of your life –</u>

Checklist in order:

1. Determine are you going to do it yourself or are you going to hire a coach.

2. Determine your values – what is most important about money to you?

3. Write out all your goals and write the dollar amounts, the dates to achieve, their priority and the benefits you will get from them.

4. Organize all your financial papers.

5. Create your gap analysis.

6. Create your initial plan.

7. Create your list of actions.

8. Implement your plan.

9. Create your system of measurement and management.

10. Adjust your plan as your life and the economic environment change.

11. Focus on your progression, not perfection.

12. Send us an email or letter to tell us about how this book has helped you improve your financial life.

If you wish to contact Mr. Himmler, you can write to:

Integrated Asset Management, LLC

560 COMMUNICATIONS PARKWAY

SARASOTA, FLORIDA 34240

You can also access many of the resources

and our "Women Only" blog by going to the following

addresses:

women.liverichstaywealthy.com

www.liverichstaywealthy.com

If you want to receive a trial subscription, you can send an email to csm@iamllc.biz. We will send you a weekly market commentary, in addition to a quarterly "Money Tips" newsletter (by email only). The subscription is free for the first year.

You can also listen to Mr. Himmler on his daily radio show. It is recorded live on Monday mornings between 9:00 a.m. and 10:00 a.m. EST and replayed each weekday on WTMY 1280 AM radio (Sarasota, Florida); then again on 1490 AM radio between 5:00 p.m. and 6:00 p.m. You can access this by going to www.wtmy.com or by going to our website at www.iamllc.biz.

There is no challenge too great

for those who have the will and the heart

to make it happen.

The LIVE RICH & STAY WEALTHY

EDUCATIONAL CLASS

Now you can attend the LIVE RICH & STAY WEALTHY EDUCATIONAL CLASSES where you can see the techniques and strategies in this book illustrated and expanded upon!

You can access the LIVE RICH STAY WEALTHY educational weekend by going to www.liverichstaywealthy.com. If you do not have internet access you can call us at 800-983-LRSW-(5779).

Appendix

Look for other books written by Kenneth Himmler, Sr.:

Live Rich and Stay Wealthy for Retirees Only

(Due out in fall of 2006)

Advanced Financial Strategies for Retirees Only

(Due out in spring of 2007)

Books I recommend:

Millionaire Women Next Door, Thomas J Stanley

Live with passion, Anthony Robbins

Values based financial planning, Bill Bacharach

Think and Grow Rich, Napoleon Hill

Finish Rich Workbook, David Bach

Start Late Finish Rich, David Bach

Smart Couples Finish Rich, David Bach

The Automatic Millionaire, David Bach

12 Choices that Lead to Your Success, David Cottrell

Last Chance to Get it Right, J.Thomas Moore

Money without Matrimony, Sheryl Garrett

Buffettology, Mary Buffett and David Clark

The Art of Asset Allocation, David M. Darst

Investing for Cowards, Fred Siegel

Efficient Asset Management, Richard O. Michaud

The Richest Man in Babylon, George S. Clayson

Rich Dad Poor Dad, Robert Kiyosaki

The Essential Buffett, Robert G. Hagstrom

The Frugal Senior, Rich Gray

Websites I recommend:

Morningstar.com

Yahoo.com/finance

Personalfund.com

MoneyguidePro.com

Quicken.com

QuantumOnline.com

FinancialFreedom.com

PUBLISHED BOOKS BY KENNETH HIMMLER, SR.

LIVE RICH
&
STAY WEALTHY

For Women Only

PASS IT ON...

Kenneth Himmler, Sr.

CEP, CRPC, CFS, BCE

LIVE RICH & STAY WEALTHY
liverichstaywealthy.com
1-800-983-LRSW (5779)

LIVE RICH
&
STAY WEALTHY

For Retirees Only

Kenneth Himmler, Sr.

CEP, CRPC, CFS, BCE

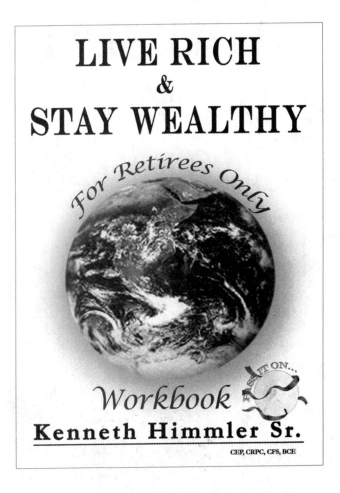

LIVE RICH & STAY WEALTHY
liverichstaywealthy.com
1-800-983-LRSW (5779)

PUBLISHED BOOKS BY KENNETH HIMMLER, SR.

LIVE RICH
&
STAY WEALTHY

For Physicians Only

PASS IT ON...

Kenneth Himmler, Sr.

CEP, CRPC, CFS, BCE

LIVE RICH & STAY WEALTHY
liverichstaywealthy.com
1-800-983-LRSW (5779)

PUBLISHED BOOKS BY KENNETH HIMMLER, SR.

LIVE RICH
&
STAY WEALTHY

For Contractors Only

PASS IT ON...

Kenneth Himmler, Sr.

CEP, CRPC, CFS, BCE